Values in America

EDITED
BY

DONALD N. BARRETT

Contributors:
Clyde Kluckhohn
Joseph P. Fitzpatri
Bernard Berelson

UNIVERSIT

Values

in

America

illiam L. Kolb   *Robin M. Williams, Jr.*   *John J. Kane*
illiam H. Form   *John A. Hutchison*   *Joseph H. Fichter*
homas J. Stritch

F NOTRE DAME PRESS   •   1 9 6 1

CONTENTS

Preface vii

1 INTRODUCTION

Value Problems and Present
Contributions • *Donald N. Barrett* . . . 1

2 ANALYSIS OF VALUES IN BEHAVIORAL SCIENCE

The Study of Values • *Clyde Kluckhohn* . . 17

Values, Determinism and
Abstraction • *William L. Kolb* 47

3 VALUES AND EDUCATION IN AMERICA

Values and Modern Education in the United
States • *Robin M. Williams, Jr.* . . . 57

Questions of Value Choice in
Education • *John J. Kane* 83

4 VALUES AND AMERICAN ECONOMIC LIFE

Individualism in American
Industry • *Joseph P. Fitzpatrick* . . . 91

Toward Re-evaluation of Individualism in
Industry • *William H. Form* 111

41526

5 VALUES AND RELIGION IN AMERICA

American Values in the Perspective
of Faith • *John A. Hutchison* 121

Religious Values, A Sociological
Perspective • *Joseph H. Fichter* 137

6 VALUES AND MASS COMMUNICATIONS
IN AMERICA

The Great Debate on Cultural
Democracy • *Bernard Berelson* 147

Communications Criticism and Artistic
Change • *Thomas J. Stritch* 171

Bibliography 177

PREFACE

More than fifty years ago Emile Durkheim made a distinction between *jugements de valeur* and *jugements de réalité*. This distinction highlights the present concern among behavioral scientists with the problems of definition, identification, classification and analysis of values. Amidst this concern, which has grown considerably since 1950, the Department of Sociology of the University of Notre Dame invited a number of distinguished social scientists to participate in a frank and open discussion of their thinking on values. By use of the symposium and seminar techniques this group attempted to explore, develop, and criticize the "reality" of values in America.

The choice of substantive areas for discussion was dictated largely by three considerations: 1) the growing interest of Americans in the particular contributions of social scientists to issues of the day; 2) the special competence of the participants by reason of their writing and research; 3) the location of basic differences of viewpoints among behavioral scientists which appeared to need confrontation and dialogue. With the benefit of hindsight it can now be said that both the choice of areas and the choice of participants had the virtue of producing constructive "clash" and deepening insight in regard to the value mainsprings of America. No pretense is made that the areas chosen are exclusively crucial, nor that the discussions are exhaustive. Yet, as significant evidence, it should be noted that the planned periods of relaxation between our meetings were also filled with rich and persistent exchanges among the participants and among the auditors.

Each of the five main sessions consisted of a major presentation, followed immediately by a formal critique and an extended period of informal interchange. In the light of the fruitfulness of the total, it seems unfortunate that only the formal aspects can be presented here. The introduction, "Value Problems and

Present Contributions," was not an original part of the symposium, but has been added to cast light on some of the basic issues and ideas throughout. Neither full summary, nor totally "new directions," this introductory essay endeavors to identify many of the questions around which much of the formal and informal argument revolved.

Many thanks are due the main participants for their fine contributions. The generous grant from the Lilly Endowment, Inc. permitted us at the University of Notre Dame to afford the setting and opportunity for these discussions. We now trust that this publication will show the value of value-dialogue.

D. N. B.

1

Introduction

*Donald N. Barrett is
Assistant Professor of Sociology and
co-chairman of the Social Science Program,
University of Notre Dame*

Donald N. Barrett

VALUE PROBLEMS AND
PRESENT CONTRIBUTIONS

WITHOUT MUCH DISPUTE MOST PEOPLE WOULD AGREE THAT values lie at the core of life and human action. This consensus, however, only marks the beginning of the argument. Value-analysis and value-commitment (or lack thereof) have puzzled philosophers, historians, economists, sociologists and anthropologists for countless years. Yet the notion of value has seldom been made the central and explicit focus of major works in modern times. More commonly, values have gained attention under disguising rubrics, just as the psychologists' current preference for such terms as motivation, strength, drive and the like.

Only recently have certain philosophers and social scientists recognized that value may be identified, for certain purposes, with a term of much longer history, namely *bonum*. This concept occupies a large place in the works of Plato, Aristotle, Thomas Aquinas, Kant and countless others. Currently, for example, one sociologist prefers to define value in its abstract sense as "the quality of recognized desirability founded on goodness."[1] Others would lean toward conceptualizations of "pref-

[1] Paul H. Furfey (1953), p. 89.
All the footnotes in the text of this book have been abbreviated, for purposes of easier reading, so that only the author and the year his work was published is cited. Complete facts of publication for all references are included in the bibliography.

erential behavior," "criteria and standards of choice," as opposed to specifications of ends and goals which are implied in the term, *bonum*.[2] Whatever the formulation, it becomes clear at the outset of the discussion that full agreement fails. Few, however, would dissent from the principles that values are important in behavior, they concern standards of choice and the normative, and they involve some degree of commitment. From this elementary starting point the myriad paths of analysis become diverse and often contradictory.

Very often the term, value, has become inextricably associated with other terms, such as "ought" and "should." Hume's powerful argument has been persuasive in favor of the notion that passing from existential to "should" statements is completely illogical and unfounded. Since this thinking is implicit in much of the modern value literature, values have been accorded the status of items vital to human action, moral in basic nature, and separated from rationally disposed reality. Two consequences of this line of thought have followed. Unfortunately, value-propositions have been identified exclusively with ethical statements, whereas their existential character and manifold qualitative categorizations, as illustrated so clearly in Kluckhohn's essay herein, have been ignored. Also since values were assumed to be nonrationally based, they have been considered outside the pale of scientific analysis. Concurrently, however, sociologists and anthropologists have argued that all categories of value are crucial in the scientific analysis of human behavior. Comte's evolutionary scheme of the "three stages" constituted a theoretical-historical interpretation of human values. The progressively changing social and personal criteria of truth and action were successively described as theological,

[2] See Ray Lepley (1949). Even in sophisticated economics, where a specialized type of value theory has been prominent, L. M. Fraser (1937) shows that it has been used in three main senses, each with many subvariants.

metaphysical and positivistic. Much of the controversy over Tylor's initial attempt to erect a "science of culture" centered on the scientific versus nonscientific claims to value analysis, and on the invasion of the presumably sacred precincts of personality. Durkheim carried the argument further in his *Cours de Science Sociale* by saying:

> La morale est de toutes les parties de la sociologie celle qui nous attire de préférence. . . . Seulement essayerons de la traiter scientifiquement. . . . Le seul moyen de mettre fin à l'antagonisme entre la science et la morale, c'est de faire de la morale elle-même une science.[3]

Despite the rather vitriolic controversy over this position, and especially over his social determinism, as expressed in "La Determination du Fait Moral" in the *Bulletin* of the French Society of Philosophy, one of his antagonists, Simon Deploige, a Louvain Catholic, espoused the thesis that Durkheim was implicitly urging a return to Thomistic principles.[4]

The instructive significance of such controversy consists in the fact that the issues were really joined. Social scientists, philosophers and historians found a place for dialogue which could not be mistaken. Unfortunately, it seemed that disciplines were monolithically aligned one against another. True, great writers within single disciplines disagreed, but behavioral scientists at least found harmony in the position that values were proper objects of scientific study. Argument with other disciplinary exponents often turned on positivism or value relativism, but the questions and positions were clearly recognized and directly at issue. Today there tends to be more stress on "position taking" and individual argument against impersonally cited adversaries.

[3] E. Durkheim (1904).
[4] Simon Deploige (1912).

THE PRESENT CONTRIBUTION AND ISSUE

The constructive contribution of the following essays finds expression in three principles: 1) social scientists, who are in the forefront of value-analysis today, are given an opportunity to extend and modify their work in the light of the present development of value-interpretation; 2) five value areas, which are fundamental to the course of American striving, are spotlighted for open discussion; 3) the arguments of the main contributions come under direct and free criticism by competent thinkers who have devoted much time and work to value-problems. The penetrating thought represented in these essays thus attempts to fulfill the paradigm of direct dialogue. In addition, crucial points of agreement and disagreement are clearly marked by careful scientists within the behavioral science tradition. At the same moment the overflow of value-questions from social to philosophical, religious and historical domains has not been excised arbitrarily in a weak pretense of disciplinary autonomy and omniscience.

Such dialogue and constructive disagreement have special relevance today. In fact, the consuming interest in values in America since World War II has almost become a sign of the times. The goals envisioned by political and social reformers of previous centuries have largely been achieved; we have general education, greater leisure, material abundance and democratic institutions in higher degree than could reasonably be hoped for. Yet our leaders seem to grow increasingly concerned and more disposed to become self-critical, uneasy and inclined toward short-term and expedient solutions to contemporary value-conflicts. The followers, on the other hand, become skeptical and superficially sophisticated in regard to basic values. Public opinion, once the gauge of society's moral climate, often seems to swing as aimlessly as the demagnetized needle of a compass. Accustomed to corruption in high places, Americans now casually accept it in low places such as well-rigged quiz shows, tawdry culture heroes and cynical management and labor leaders. What seems unique is not that value-problems are no longer recognized. Quite the contrary, the contrasting value-allegiances in the issues surrounding Senator McCarthy, in the questions about strengths and weaknesses in our educational system, in problems concerning honesty, integrity and morality in advertising and mass communications, have all been given greater play before the public than even survival issues of the past. What appears to be new today is contained in Hutchison's question: does this interest in value-problems make a "difference" in human action?

Science, once regarded as the Prometheus of our age, now at times looks like the witless Caliban, his cave filled with nuclear bombs, the weapons of chemical and biological warfare, drugs to alter the human personality for better or worse, and endless instruments for labor saving, entertainment and "happy" living. But science has proven less than satisfactory in its solutions for major human problems. The scientists' struggle to gain a hearing before voters and leaders, their expressed concern for their responsibility over the consequences of scientific innovations, the struggle over military and civilian uses of atomic rocketry research, all combine to show that science has become seriously embroiled in important value-issues which themselves are beyond the competence of natural science.

Social scientists have not been oblivious to the seriousness of such a situation. The major difficulty, as Merton has often suggested, is to bring together two categories of contemporary workers in value-problems: those who are scientifically certain of the truth of what they are saying, although it may be miniscule or insignificant in the face of large problems; and those who are certain of the significance of what they are saying, although they are not scientifically certain of its truth. George Lundberg has charged that the reluctance to study important value-questions scientifically has arisen because of semantic confusion. Value and "ought" statements he considers to be representations of expectations, which are, in effect, predictions, e.g., he ought to be ashamed (if he were decent, civilized, etc.), or the engine ought to start (if the gasoline and ignition are both in order). The reduction of value-judgments to implicit prediction propositions is not common among social scientists, but it reflects one attempt to bridge the gap between value and existential statements, so that the question can be validly raised: *Can Science Save Us?* In contrast other social scientists have argued that Lundberg equivocates in his use of the term, "expected," between what is anticipated as the result of nature's processes and what is demanded or hoped for in terms of humanly developed standards.

In remarkably similar yet independent fashion, both F. S. C. Northrop and Jacques Maritain maintain that primitive concepts of nature and primitive postulates about nature underlie value-systems. Thus, as Kluckhohn points out, the Navaho think of the natural order as potentially harmonious and their ceremonial manifests the value placed on this concept when various rites are designed to maintain, promote or restore this potential harmony. Such beliefs, then, independent of scientific proof and cultural determination (beliefs as valued, however, thereby enter culture), may be considered a fundamental starting point in value-analysis. As soon as such beliefs go beyond speculation and become incorporated into personal and social systems as portraying objects capable of satisfying human desire, one begins to speak of values. This viewpoint of values is not necessarily concordant with the definitional assumptions of all the participants in the following discussions. However, it does serve to give grounding to three widely recognized value-principles. (1), Values must be understood as relational between evaluator and valued object. Thus, rather than concepts, values may be considered to be basically judgmental in their manifestations, e.g., this is desirable, useful, beneficial. (2), Values also admit of a greater or less strength, affective power and action commitment. The absence of all reservations and conditions is rare indeed among operational values. Also like most personal, social and cultural systems, stability does not mean that processes or changes do not occur, nor that individuals within the same system have precisely the same values. (3), Values are not identifiable coterminously with goals or beliefs, but tend to become architectonically organized criteria by which most beliefs and goals are selected. Yet, it must be noted, these same values, discovered and experienced on an approval-disapproval continuum, seldom show the rigid consistency and order of mathematical systems. Inconsistencies arise, for example, from variations in valued fundamental beliefs, from inadequate rationalization of the system, or from the many cross-pressures and ambivalences in the systems within which one participates. Out of such realistic human conditions values appear and no amount of rational systematizing, it seems, will make operational values synchronous with a perfect ordering scheme.

THE SPECIFIC VALUE-PROBLEMS

In the face of such analytic difficulties, however, social scientists consider it axiomatic that generalizations can validly be made about human action. Even inconsistencies in value-schemes may show pattern, purpose and function. What appear to us as inconsistencies do not lead to a valid inference that such values are dysfunctional in their own setting. The first of our five studies faces directly the problem of systematic analysis of inconsistencies and variations in the core values of five cultures co-existing in the same ecological area of New Mexico. Drawing from the theoretical and statistical work of F. Kluckhohn and Strodtbeck, C. Kluckhohn clearly delineates an efficient way of portraying value-variations within and across cultures. In a period of many years of research a multidimensional system of value-categories has been built up, thereby permitting deeper insight and comprehension than has been characteristic of "trait" listings and broadly generalized categorial systems. Popular terms, such as Ruth Benedict's "Apollonian" and "Dionysian" cultures, become hereby little but catchalls which obscure as much as they reveal. The problem of studying values, then, is not exclusively one of observation and validation, but one of *verstehen* and interpretation.

To facilitate this process further, Kluckhohn has taken a linguistic model to explore the usefulness of an extended but provisional list of value-oppositions. The five culture groups in New Mexico are hypothetically asked to respond to such questions as: do you give priority to orderliness (lawfulness) in the universe as opposed to chance or caprice; is nature (including inanimate, animate and supernatural) threatening or beneficent (good-evil) ; is the world to be thought of as a single manifold or as segmented into two or more spheres in which different principles prevail? Then an attempt is made to determine what combinations are likely and unlikely, possible and impossible, in a value-matrix, by some very interesting tests of complementarity and implication of these values. Kolb, however, takes forthright issue with the "maximum level of abstraction" on which these value-categories appear to be placed. It becomes quite proper, then, to raise questions concerning the potential fruitfulness of using such abstract polarities, especially in the search for the rapid development of value-theory which has thus far escaped social scientists. Another question raised in criticism points to the apparent credence given to determinism and nonresponsibility by such levels and types of conceptualizations. The problems and differences of viewpoints are nonetheless clearly and candidly posed here. Max Weber has insisted on a caution quite apropos:

> Remember that we, in a way, structure reality by a set of concepts — we feel that regular recurrence of certain causal relationships are really all that matter — yet the epistemology

of any culture and the objects selected from the infinity of valuable things are but small proportion of what could be so analyzed.[5]

Max Weber's view is reflected in Robin Williams' essay on values and education, where the point is made that "what is taught is not just an automatic reflection of an objective world — 'objective' in the sense that no preferences are involved and no criteria of selection applied." "Education cannot avoid dealing with values, either in the case of evaluation of the world or in the case of standards in terms of which judgments of desirability are made." When this finds complement in the educational objective of changing its participants, then an elaboration of the dominant value-themes in American society and their manifestations in our educational dilemmas and conflicts is most to the point. Williams finds that many of our educational dilemmas derive from the basic variations in values and beliefs of our culture. The dilemmas concerning the model of educated person to be taught, the emphasis on the creation of knowledge with its attendant tension and conflict compared to simple transmission of knowledge, and concerning the distance taken to protect students against failure; all involve stress, compromises and continuing debate over value-choices. Just as Kluckhohn uses extensive field material, so Williams draws upon field data from sociological and psychological research, especially the Cornell Values Studies. Much that is contrary to received opinion and popular dictum is revealed here, not the least of which is the conclusion that "college students are not anything like the uniform mass of contented and unquestioning conformists they are sometimes represented to be." This absence of pure and uncritical conformity and ethical robotism should arouse serious second thoughts in peace-and-security-con-

[5] See "Objectivity in Social Science and Social Policy," essay 2 in Max Weber (1949), p. 76.

scious administrations and faculties, as well as Cassandra-type exponents of the "mass society" theme. Interestingly enough, religious institutions of higher learning, which are often considered to be ultimate breaks against the tide of conformity and materialism, are not effecting a student mold different from other institutions, according to the limited study of John Kane. It becomes clear, then, as Kluckhohn has insisted, that simplified value-models of whole cultures or institutions are both inadequate and misleading.

Kluckhohn has endeavored to analyze "core values" and in similar fashion Williams speaks of "dominant value-themes." In his examination of economic life in America Fitzpatrick takes it for granted that individualism has been our traditional "central value." Competition, freedom, success and equal opportunity were considered subordinate to individualism, which is defined as the "idea that everything must be done to give each individual the freedom to achieve the fulfillment of which he is capable." Under the impact of the modal values which Kluckhohn and Williams have termed "active mastery over the environment," American industry, according to Fitzpatrick, has changed structurally from small to large, highly organized units, to a white collar society, to great industrial responsibility for influencing domestic and foreign policies. The question is not whether individualism can survive in the face of mass work-groups, but whether the defect is in the rationalization of our values. In refreshing contrast to much of today's literature, the thesis is adduced that individualism and freedom must be recognized and now confined to group action, and in this way the worker makes his valuable contribution, rather than as an isolated individual. Freely chosen, individually satisfying and responsible group effort thus achieves the individual's self-interest, as well as collective goals. Our economic system in this perspective differs vitally from the Russian and has rationalization far beyond the unfounded boast of greater productivity. In the face of this optimistic viewpoint Form disagrees fundamentally, suggesting both that perhaps individualism has never been characteristic of most workers, if we are to judge from the evidence, and that few today place national over business interests. Constructively, however, the criticism points to the potential values of "multiple determination" of all economic and political policies by major economic groups. This, in turn, could protect individual dignity and freedom of the worker in ways amenable to large group participation. In this manner responsible disagreement and understanding of American values grow by scientific dialogue.

Such a felicitous assessment of the situation, however, may not be too accurate, if we are to judge by the criteria delineated by Hutchison. The ambiguity, subjectivity and hidden assumptions in value-analysis become clearly crucial in his examination of "American Values in the Perspective of Faith." Is it true that theologians and other academicians do not use the same language on values? Yet religious values may be considered to refer to ultimate concern, basic and unqualified commitment. In Hutchison's view, then, the ground for Form's "personalism" and Kluckhohn's "unity" value in a culture may be found in the unification of personality by way of religious values. The changes, inconsistencies and variations in educational, industrial and other cultural values, as described by the previous authors, thus encourage a most serious question relative to the depth of America's ultimate valuation. Strong nationalism, a form of modern tribalism, can be interpreted as incompatible with a biblical God. Hutchison further insists that the bulging churches in America largely reflect national conformity, custom and insurance against the possibility of a real divinity, rather than enduring primal values. "He (the American) is a decent, moderately public-spirited citizen, a family man, and a churchman . . . a hollow man." The contemporary American, therefore, is considered ill-equipped to make the vital political, economic and social decisions of which Fitzpatrick and Williams speak.

Several contrary arguments are presented by Fichter and a most crucial one refers to the previous definition of religion in basically psychological, individual terms. The social and cultural manifestations of faith through group activities, social roles and shared values encompass the reality of religion in important degree too. Americanization of religion then becomes comprehensible. If religion and culture are considered separate and different, the natural analytic view falls into a criticism of the apartheid or of the failure of a culture to accept religion's ideally static sacredness. If religion and culture are considered to be overlapping, then logical sociological perspective recognizes that each culture expresses its religion differently. Of singular interest are Fichter's more optimistic arguments that "there is no need to apologize for our typical American virtues, or to suppose that these virtues simply cannot be spiritually or religiously motivated."

"By their fruits you shall know them" has been used by Hutchison for analysis of religious values in America, but its applicability to the current debate about the impact of our system of mass communication has special timeliness. Berelson indicates that the critics and defenders of the mass media have often not based their arguments on constructive and real issues. Should the media give the public what it wants or what someone thinks is good for it on ethical or artistic grounds? The clashes of argument on the impact of the media on values, their reflection of American values, its struggle for economic and social success have been provocatively put into the mouths of three persons in direct debate — Academicus, Empiricus and Practicus. Among many others here, we find Dwight Mac-Donald, who reasons that what the Germans call *kitsch* or junk culture tends to drive out high culture and that since mass culture is so easy to produce, it overwhelms by its very quantity, and people's tastes sink to that of the least sensitive and most ignorant.[6]

But the difference in Berelson's work lies in the fact that there is immediate rebuttal and counterargument, such as the evidence that little proof of value-change under the impact of the media has been forthcoming. The critics seem to want change and stability at the same time and they are wont to accuse the mass media, whereas the value-generating institutions of family, school and church tend to be ignored.

In discussion Stritch agrees that all sides of the debate must get together and find a common denominator, but this appears to be the basic problem. We are notoriously a friendly, gregarious people, but we are not accustomed to strengthen our beliefs and values by debate and trial. In constructive vein the suggestion is made that much of fine art is transmuted folk art; and it is the responsibility of the creative minds in our culture to effect this change, rather than remain within a small and protected academic or artistic environment. Even this cannot be accepted as the solution or panacea, for, like all participants in this discussion, he agrees that the debate must continue and be taken seriously.

TOWARD CONSTRUCTIVE RESOLUTIONS

On this tenor of analysis we see that serious students of values in America have become concerned over our commitment to and rationalization of values. In the encounter, consensus has been achieved that greater engagement and constructive debate have special propriety. In contrast with much of our popular, pessimistic writing most of the authors here have concluded that mass culture, secularization, the social ethic

[6] See "A Theory of Mass Culture," in Bernard Rosenberg and David Manning White (1957), pp. 59-73. It is also noteworthy that of the 49 essays contained in this volume only seven are favorable to American tastes and values.

and homogenization of values are not balanced descriptions of America. Works hypercritical of our values tend to gain a ready audience, but this cannot become a governing criterion for scientific analysis. The humanitarian inspiration among many social critics has taken a negative mold which tends to gloss over the positive and optimistic values. Perhaps along with David Riesman and David Bell the present discussion constitutes a sign of more cumulative and favorable study of the mainsprings of American behavior. We may also hope that the dialogue presented here will help fulfill the ambition expressed by the Cornell value-study group:

> The concept 'value' supplies a point of convergence for the various specialized social sciences, and is a key concept for the integration with studies in the humanities. Value is potentially a bridging concept which can link together many diverse specialized studies — from the experimental psychology of perception to the analysis of political ideologies, from budget studies in economics to aesthetic theory and philosophy of language, from literature to race riots. . . .

This convergence of critics and disciplines can immeasurably aid in the definition, validation, categorization and interpretation of American values. Although "value" may well be a "spongy concept," fraught with hidden meanings and assumptions, it still seems worthwhile to say that what is needed today is a focus for America's immense energies, a system of values capable of restoring coherence to its inner life and a truly human meaning to its art, its scientific accomplishments and to its economic, social and political decisions. In a democracy the effective way of struggling toward this end is by taking the debate on values seriously.

2

Analysis of Values
in Behavioral Science

*Clyde Kluckhohn was
Professor of Anthropology, Harvard University, 1946-1960;
authority on the Navaho Indians; helped organize and
directed (1947-1954) the Russian Research Center;
published works in physical, social and archeological
branches of Anthropology; held a number of government
positions in a full-time or advisory capacity;
president of the American Anthropological Association, 1947;
among his many publications:* Mirror for Man, *1949,
and* The Navaho *(with Dorothea Leighton), 1947;
very active in many other organizations, often with positions and
honors bestowed; died in 1960 to the great loss of all
who knew him and his work.*

Clyde Kluckhohn

THE STUDY

OF VALUES[1]

ONE OF THE SIGNS OF THE TIMES IS THE GREAT INCREASE in the amount of research time given by behavioral scientists to the study of values. Since a number of able and wide-ranging treatments have recently appeared (e.g., Kolb, 1957; Maslow, 1959), I shall limit myself to four interrelated topics:

1) A conception of values from the standpoint of behavioral science;
2) Brief remarks upon selected aspects of a research project on values in five Southwestern cultures;
3) A prolegomena to a new type of value analysis;
4) A partial application of this scheme to the five cultures.

THE CONCEPTION OF VALUES

In the broadest sense, behavioral scientists may usefully think of values as abstract and perduring standards, which are held by an individual and/or a specified group to transcend the impulses of the moment and ephemeral situations. From the psychological point of view, a value may be defined as that

[1] This paper is an outgrowth of two previous publications (Kluckhohn, 1956; 1959). Some of the work expressed here is developed in those sources and gratitude is expressed to the Chicago University Press and Toronto University Press to re-use these portions. However, as well as editorial revision, there has been much addition, subtraction, and sub-stantive change. A significant portion of the work here is a contribution from the Values Project, supported by the Rockefeller Foundation through its Division of Social Sciences.

aspect of motivation which is referable to standards, personal or cultural, that do not arise solely out of an immediate situation and the satisfaction of needs and primary drives. Concretely, of course, values are always manifested in the verbal and motor behavior of individuals — including what is *not* said and *not* done. There are research purposes for which it is necessary to focus upon personal values as such, though such personal values are ordinarily no more than the idiosyncratic variants of values which may, by abstraction, be attributed to a group or to a culture or subculture. However, not everything culturally valued constitutes a value in the meaning I intend but only those principles on the highest level of generality from which more specific norms and acts of valuation can be derived. Henceforth in this paper I shall be dealing solely with cultural values in this sense.

A value is a selective orientation toward experience, implying deep commitment or repudiation, which influences the ordering of "choices" between possible alternatives in action. These orientations may be cognitive and expressed verbally or merely inferable from recurrent trends in behavior. (One merit of the study of values by behavioral scientists is that values are drawn out into the realm of the explicit.) A value, though conditioned by biological and social necessity, is in its particulate form arbitrary and conventional. Values are related to and dependent upon nature, but they are not "in nature" in the same fashion as, say, mass and energy. Specifically cultural values (both *seriatim* and even more in culturally specific combinations) contribute as much to cultural definitions of the situation as do each culture's existential beliefs.

Behavior oriented by a value or by values constitutes one class of preferential behavior. But such behavior belongs to the category regarded as "desirable" or "undesirable" by the group with which the individual identifies — not to that of acts which a person simply desires or does not desire. With values there is always the implication of conflict or tension. Mere desiring does not instate a value; the desires have, as it were, to be criticized and compared. Sometimes, to be sure, the two categories of desired and desirable merge in the life-experience of wise or fortunate individuals. A saying is attributed to Confucius: "In my old age I found that I had to do what I wanted to do and wanted to do what I had to do." Nevertheless both introspection and observation tell us forcefully that the areas of the desirable and the desired are not always — or even often — coextensive.

This circumstance sometimes escapes behavioral scientists. When I talk to clinical psychologists, they frequently say, "Oh, yes, I know what you mean by 'value.' It is what we call 'need' or 'cathexis.'" And the experimental psychologists will similarly remark, "That is what we refer to as 'drive strength.'" If this equation of concepts were adequate to our data, we should — on the principle of Occam's razor — simply drop the term, "value." Yet it is an induction from ordinary experience that, on occasion, all of us behave in ways that go contrary, in whole or in part, to our "wants" or "desires" as they arise in the biological organism at that moment. The existence of the value-element may transform the desired into the not-desired or the ambivalently desired. Disvalued activity is constantly cathected. A cathexis is an impulse. A value or values restrain or canalize impulses in terms of what a group has defined as wider or more enduring goods. The "desirable" becomes a distinctive component in motivation. The uniqueness of the presence of values, a somewhat separate, special area in human life, different in kind from other cognitive and affective influences, is almost universally recognized or "felt" as such.

"Needs," for instance, and "values" certainly have mutual implications. The few elemental needs that all human beings share have a recognizable similarity across cultures, though differently weighted and varyingly formulated in detail. On the other hand, some needs (for example for food and water) are merely biological givens. The question of value arises only when the possibility of selection in accord with abstract standards exists or is held to exist. When certain desired and nutritious foods are tabooed or when others are arbitrarily considered "better," then and only then are we in the realm of value. "Values" designate preferences that cannot be derived solely from the existence of needs. Some "choices" do not involve value-elements but only need-elements. Specific bodily deprivations and gratifications may be relevant to a great many values but do not themselves constitute value phenomena. Needs and values are not thereby identified. Moreover, their relationship may be circular. Psychological needs are created by cultural values; it remains true that some values are in a very general way responses to basic human needs. But values are not to be identified with needs any more than they are with objects. Value is a relational rather than an entity concept. Value rests in a nexus of relationships.

Values, then, are images formulating positive or negative action commitments, a set of hierarchically ordered prescriptions and proscriptions. Without a hierarchy of values human behavior could be described by a list of instincts and a probabilistic calculus. Human life would become a sequence of reactions to unconfigurated stimuli. Values are standards which complicate the individual's satisfactions of his immediate wishes and needs. They take distinctive forms in different cultures, tend to persist tenaciously through time, and are not mere random outcomes of conflicting human desires.

I follow the position taken recently by the famous geneticist, H. J. Muller: ". . . values are as legitimate a subject of scientific investigation as any other phenomena pertaining to human beings." I shall not here beg in any way the question as to whether or not the "truth" of value-judgments can be settled or partly settled by scientific enquiry. I assert only that values are cultural and psychological facts of a certain type which can be discovered and analyzed with as much detachment as at least some other types of cultural and psychological facts. Fundamentally, one does the same as in other areas of behavior: one listens to what people say and for what they fail to say; one observes what they do and don't do; one gets at what they are unable or unwilling to say by projective tests, depth interviews, and other techniques.

Values can be described with some precision. Their place in the structure of the culture and the workings of the society can be established.

VALUES IN FIVE SOUTHWESTERN CULTURES

During the years 1949-1954 the Laboratory of Social Relations of Harvard University carried on a multidisciplinary investigation of the values of five cultures (Mormon, Texan, Spanish-American, Zuni, and Navaho) coexisting in the same ecological area of New Mexico. Empirical studies ranged from cross-cultural interviewing and observation on nausea, to the use of a tachistoscope to discover whether perception of closure varied culturally, to child-play with projective toys and drawings; from social history and humor to the aesthetics of music and the graphic arts. Some research, to be sure, was more squarely within the framework of values as traditionally conceived: a comparison of the values of Navahos who had served in World War II with those of their close relatives of about the same age who had not had this experience; an analysis of myths which dissected out relationships between values, social organization, and other variables; an enquiry by interview into the tacit premises of an ethical system; an analysis of Zuni quarrels and "legal" cases in value terms. In all investigations field workers were asked to pay particular attention to certain "operational indices" of which the following are representative:

1) Manifestations of approval or disapproval in word or deed.
2) Differential effort exhibited toward the attainment of ends, access to means, or acquisition of modes of behavior.
3) Behavior (and hypothetical behavior) in "choice" and especially crisis situations.

Let me say a little about one specific piece of research.[2] This involves a theory of value-orientations which emphasizes the "built-in" variation in each value system and a methodology for ascertaining the value-profile of each culture and for comparing in standardized ways different value-profiles and their internal variations. (F. Kluckhohn and Strodtbeck, 1959.) Florence Kluckhohn's theory of value-orientations singles out five crucial questions common to all human groups:

1) What is the character of innate human nature? (Human-Nature Orientation)
2) What is the relation of man to nature (supernature)? (Man-Nature Orientation)
3) What is the temporal focus of human life? (Time Orientation)
4) What is the modality of human activity? (Activity Orientation)
5) What is the modality of man's relationship to other men? (Relational Orientation).

Perhaps the greatest theoretical innovation in Florence Kluckhohn's work upon value-orientations is that her theory permits — indeed demands — a multidimensional analysis. Previous characterizations of core values were too static, too absolutistic, took far too little account of variation. Thus for Ruth Benedict, Zuni culture was "Apollonian" and Kwakiutl culture was "Dionysian." Such sweeping labels are, at best, very rough impressionistic catchalls. They ignore the countercurrents. All

---

[2] For a complete bibliography of published work see E. Z. Vogt and J. M. Roberts (1960).

ethnographers know, for example, that there are at Zuni patterned behaviors which, in Benedict's own terms, are unmistakably "Dionysian." These she either fails to mention or, in effect, tries to explain away. Moreover, Benedict largely fails to take account of the fact that cultural values are varyingly weighted in different kinds of activities and for persons occupying particular statuses or playing particular roles.

Florence Kluckhohn, on the other hand, postulates systematic variation in the whole realm of cultural phenomena and not least in the value sector. There is both permitted and required variation. As regards the value-orientations specifically, she assumes that each of the three positions for the five orientations will be represented in every culture. What needs to be determined is the rank ordering. Spanish-Americans, for instance, were found to have these profiles of rank orders:

Relational:	1. Individualistic	2. Lineal	3. Collateral
Time:	1. Present	2. Future	3. Past
Man-Nature:	1. Subjugated	2. Over-nature	3. With-nature

The profile of rank orders for the same value-orientations of the Texan neighbors of the Spanish-American village comes out this way:

Relational:	1. Individualistic	2. Collateral	3. Lineal
Time:	1. Future	2. Present	3. Past
Man-Nature:	1. Over	2. With	3. Subjugated

As a matter of fact, the detailed statistical analysis of F. Kluckhohn and Strodtbeck reveals still finer shadings. Thus they demonstrate that the Spanish-Americans are only *slightly* more individualistically than lineally oriented in their dominant position for the relational value-orientation.

A comparison in terms of profiles is immensely more just to the rich variability of actuality — *and* to the essential nature of value-systems — than to rest with saying: "Spanish-Americans are individualistic, present-time oriented, and regard themselves as subjugated to nature, whereas Texans are individualistic, future-oriented, and intent upon mastering nature." The contrasts in the various second- and third-order positions in each case sensitively reveal important information. One hardly needs belabor the advantages of the profiles versus single portmanteau words such as "Dionysian" or "Apollonian."

Another outstanding feature of the theory which I can only mention is a new outlook which it provides for a model of value-change and of cultural change generally. There is that sort of change summed up in Desmoulins' phrase: *Plus ça change, plus c'est la même chose.* It is likewise generally recognized that fundamental values alter slowly — in the overwhelming majority of cases. But — and this is the new point — basic value-shifts occur when external pressures impinge upon the already existent variation in the system. The systematic variation always contains the potentiality for change but remains dormant or latent[3] until environmental events or intensified contacts with other cultures bring a second- or third-order position into dominance. If this be correct, we escape the puzzling mystique of "immanent causation." My wife had studied the values of the Spanish-American village fifteen years before the field work of the Values Project was carried out. At this time the lineal orientation was definitely dominant. By 1951 it had become, by a shade, subordinate to the individualistic orientation. This shift she had predicted in 1936 and specified the variant individuals who would be the bearers of the trend.[4]

---

[3] "Dormant or latent" only from the point of view of leading to value shifts. When a society and its value-system are in a state of equilibrium the variant values are active but mainly supportive of the dominant values.

[4] The work of F. Kluckhohn-Strodtbeck also made a significant methodological contribution. A value-choice instrument was developed to test the validity of the advance predictions by "experts" on each of the five cultures. The application of this instrument to random samples in the

AN APPROACH TO VALUE-ANALYSIS

Finally, I want to sketch for you another approach which is far less thoroughly worked through empirically and theoretically than the one we have just been considering. Yet I think it to be promising both as a supplement to the other line of attack and perhaps also as posing issues which, while overlapping, are somewhat wider and somewhat different. The two approaches share many points of departure, but this one arises immediately out of anthropological linguistics and does not rely at all upon statistical formulae. It is a form of pattern analysis, a trial at transferring to value-culture some procedures which have been applied with great success to linguistic culture.

Linguists, in their elegant analyses of one aspect of culture, have found it extremely useful to set up a series of distinctive contrasts or oppositions, usually binary, which serve to identify each separate phoneme (sound class distinctive in that language). A "lump" or "bundle" of such "distinctive features" defines a phoneme. In its simplest form, the process is like a specialized version of the "twenty questions game." Thus one may ask, "Is the phoneme vocalic? Yes or no?" In Russian, eleven such questions will identify each phoneme uniquely. In the French phonemic system, the binary oppositions are the following: vowel-consonant, nasal-oral, saturated-diluted, grave-acute, tense-lax, and continuous-intercepted. While the particular principles or distinctive features and their combinations vary from one phonemic system to another, a total list of the oppositions utilized in known languages would not exceed twenty.

There are grounds for supposing that a similar approach will yield good results with other aspects of culture, including cultural values. Human nature and the human situation are such that there are some fundamental questions of value upon

cultures showed that, on the whole, the earlier predictions stood up very well. The economy of time and effort achieved by this method warrants special consideration by future scholars and researchers on values.

which all cultures have taken a position, explicit or implicit. As in the case of language, the foci or structure-points are largely supplied by the limits and potentialities given by the physical world, human biology, and social requirements. With language, the properties of sound waves, the anatomy and physiology of the speech organs, and social (communicative) needs constrain the range of variation. With values, such unavoidable facts as dependence upon the external environment, birth and death, and social relatedness make value "choices" in these areas inescapable. Nor is the range of loci for selection or indeed of possible selections at each locus unconstrained. Just as all phonemic systems include nasals, stops, and sibilants, so all value-systems place their weightings, for instance, on the desirable relations to nature, other individuals, and the self within a describable set of alternatives.

The entities of value-culture do not have the all-or-none character of a simple physical event like the phones found in language culture. Rather, they seem to have the character of weightings or emphases that are, on the whole, dominant in the culture. Even here there are parallels. A language or a phonemic system is, after all, a high order abstraction. Concretely, each person's speech is an idiodialect, and even this varies through time and between situations. Similarly, some individuals or groups may accept the variant rather than the dominant cultural values. They may reject some or many of the core values. To those values, whether dominant or variant, that they do accept each individual gives an interpretation and a coloring that is more or less private. It nevertheless remains meaningful to abstract common elements both in language and in values.

By using the linguistic technique of seeing which distributions are complementary, coincident, incorporating and overlapping, anthropologists may be able to answer the questions that are at the heart of the principles of selectivity which determine the distinctiveness of each culture. Which combinations of value-emphases are "impossible?" Which are very rare and probably due to exceptional circumstances? Which are so frequent as to be predictable? On which is no guess justified one way or the other? This particular task will indeed involve counting, but the initial determination of the contrasting pairs is more likely to follow the linguistic experience. Once a linguist is certain that in one instance a glottalized and a non-glottalized voiceless stop at the same articulatory position are in complementary distribution — or produce variation in the meaning of a morpheme — he knows he has two distinct phonemes. In addition, he knows that there is an overwhelming likelihood that glottalization is one of the distinctive features of that language and is decisive in a number of phonemic contrasts.

Dichotomies are very slippery,[5] to be sure, and the use of them often brings about a false simplification of the phenomena. Yet they are not merely convenient. The fact that human beings have two eyes, two hands, two feet; the alternation of night and day; the existence of two sexes, and other circumstances make it almost inevitable that people tend strongly to think in terms of "either . . . or" and "yes or no." In every culture there are many paired opposites: "love and hate," "friends and enemies," and the like. Early historic religions are full of famous dualisms: Yang and Yin (comprising such opposites as heaven and earth, sun and moon, fire and cold, active and passive, strength and weakness, male and female); God and the Devil; the Zoroastrian antithesis of Truth and Lie; myths of the conflict between Order and Chaos or Light and Darkness. "Ego" and "object" are a polar pair in normal mental functioning. Hence, however

[5] For discussions of logical and empirical difficulties see Speiser (1938) and Mannoury (1950). It is also true that not all contemporary linguists accept the proposition of Jakobson and other Prague phonologists that all oppositions must be binary (Householder, 1958, pp. 406ff.). Certainly the ternary classification of F. Kluckhohn offers certain advantages. Nevertheless, on balance, the case for using two contrasting emphases makes the attempt justified.

false to the complexity of the natural world this anthropocentric two-valued logic may be, it remains true that human behavior (see Spitz, 1957) frequently takes place on the binary basis, and this propensity introduces some regularities useful for scientific analysis. The binary computer has been successfully used as an analogue to the human nervous system. No multivalued logic has thus far been very successful except at the level of formal mathematical notation.

The inventory of polar existential opposition is large: big-small, ruler-ruled, owner-owned, etc. Nature appears to be continuous, but man's judgments or nature are discontinuous: they are finally resolved into a yea or a nay. Even if a person is aware of a vast possibility of selections, the final decision comes on a "yes-or-no" basis.

I arrived by a series of successive approximations at the provisional list of value-oppositions which follows. I drew upon the broadest categories of human experience as revealed in history, philosophy, and the arts. I examined and tried out somewhat similar lists, such as those appearing in Charles Morris' *Paths of Life* and *The Open Self*. I found books and articles by E. Rothacker and H. Plessner helpful. By eliminating distinctions that appeared to be purely verbal or special instances of a wider category, I constructed a first list of dichotomous pairs which graduate students in my seminar applied to materials from a number of cultures. This led to further deletions but also to some additions. I stopped revising at the point where most judgment came fairly comfortably and where little or nothing pertaining to core values appeared to be left out.[6]

Before proceeding to the tentative list, I do want to underline my premise that the ontological status of these pairs is not

[6] No one is more conscious than I that the provisional list is neither exhaustive nor final. Further changes might indicate: 1) needed inclusion of additional pairs, e.g., scepticism-credulity; 2) some dichotomies may be equally weighted or sex-linked in various cultures.

that of true dichotomies but rather of bipolar dimensions. The two-feature oppositions are not so constituted that one empirically excludes the presence of the other in the culture, even though, in a formal sense, the relationship is in some cases that of contraries. Sufficient materials analyzed in terms of the complementary and other distributions may show that there are both "contradictories" (one negates the other) and "contraries" (one excludes the other). These and similar questions can eventually be settled by rigorous application of set theory, but I believe the categories are so crude at present as to make this application premature right now.

It will be noted that some of the emphases relate to existential dimensions. As Northrop and others have argued, basic values are always tied to and dependent upon a culture's conceptions of the ultimate nature of things. All fundamental views of nature have implications for the value system.

VALUE-OPPOSITIONS

Determinate-Indeterminate. This contrast hinges upon the priority given to orderliness (lawfulness) in the universe as opposed to chance or caprice or any factor or factors that make prediction or control impossible *in principle*. A "mechanistic" emphasis does not necessarily make human effort, including ritual effort, irrelevant. On the contrary, as the cases of Navaho, Zuni, and many other nonliterate cultures show, this conception may heighten the amount and detail of ritual behavior, both negative and positive. The Epicurean and Buddhist instances show in other ways how this contrast is not that between theism and atheism. Nor is this exclusively the polarity between "fatalism" or "predetermination" versus "free will" or "accident." Rather, the essential contrast is between a state of affairs conceived as operating in consistent and lawful fashion and one where an indeterminism (of whatever sort) reigns. The former case may eventuate in the outlook of Western science as stated

by Karl Pearson or in the attempt to control events by supernatural techniques or in "fatalistic" acceptance. The latter,
however, may also have a "fatalistic" toning in a different sense:
resignation to "taking things as they come" without rhyme or
reason. The indeterminate emphasis may also take the form of
extreme voluntarism (either human or divine), since nothing
is held to be completely determined or determinable. The outcome in the case of both alternatives will depend upon how this
emphasis is juxtaposed with other cultural emphases. Nevertheless, I believe this particular binary opposition to be of absolutely crucial significance.

Unitary-Pluralistic. Is the world, including human life,
thought of as a single manifold or as segmented into two or
more spheres in which different principles prevail? At first
glance this contrast might appear to be a special case of the first.
Certainly it would seem logically probable that the unitary
emphasis would be likely to be found where the mechanistic
emphasis dominates. But there are innumerable instances of
"mechanistic" cultures exhibiting the familiar dualisms of "sacred and profane," "mind and body," not merely as categories
in a larger whole but as altogether separate realms governed by
distinct "laws" and with one construed as more permanent and
superior to the other. Conversely, the ancient Greeks who believed in ineluctable laws had a profoundly unitary conception
of life.

Evil-Good. Cultures ordinarily attribute to inanimate nature,
to supernatural beings, and to human nature properties that are
positively or negatively toned. Nature is threatening or beneficent; the supernaturals may or may not be effectively propi-
tiated; human nature is basically good or evil. To be sure, the
judgments often—or perhaps usually—come in somewhat mixed
or qualified form, but I suspect that one polarity or the other
usually stands out. Emphasis upon "good" does not mean in the
least that the problem of evil is ignored. Thus the Zunis show

considerable fear of the evil intentions of individuals and groups outside the intimate household; they likewise are concerned with disaster from events of nature. Yet the Zunis still conceive the cosmos as fundamentally a good place. All things are in the final analysis benevolent functioning parts of a universal, timeless order. The dead join a legion of beneficent beings who stand ready to help those living at Zuni. The Navaho, on the other hand, who exhibit no more fear of witches and natural events than do the Zuni, nevertheless conceive the order of the universe as "evil" in the sense that it is dominantly harsh and implacable. The dead are neither happy nor beneficent. Dominance of the "evil" aspect in men or gods or both commonly leads to "the tragic sense of life," but this may also result from a belief in man's being at the mercy of the caprices of impersonal nature. Whether cultures take what Florence Kluckhohn calls the subjugated-to-nature, the in-nature, or the over-nature position depends upon how the mechanistic-indeterminate, good-evil, and active-acceptant value emphases are combined. Other combinations lead to dominance of optimistic, pessimistic, or resigned attitudes as dominant.

Individual-Group. Is the individual or some collectivity or collectivities (family, clan, local group, clique, occupational group, or tribe or nation) given priority? Is the individual a means to the ends of some collectivity or vice versa?

Self-Other.[7] This refers to the relative emphasis placed upon egoism and altruism. The "other" consists in other individuals

---

[7] I feel that this dichotomy has given rather good results in practice. Conceptually, however, it may be questioned whether it is valid across cultural lines. As Dorothy Lee (1959, p. 174) says, there are cultures where the self and the other are differentiated but not mutually exclusive:

The self contains some of the other, participates in the other and is in part contained within the other. By this I do not mean what usually goes under the name of empathy. I mean rather that where such a concept of the self is operative, self-interest and other-interest are not clearly distinguished; so that what I do for my own good is necessarily also good for my unit, the surround, whether this is my rather than in various solidary collectivities. For example, loyalty and devotion—at some expense to the interests of the self—are enjoined toward wife, children, and other relatives as persons rather than as members of a family entity. Or the emphasis may be directed primarily toward friends or occupational or ritual associates or to a god or gods. In any case the needs of the self are placed as high or low in reference to the needs of others (*as individual personalities*).

Autonomy-Dependence. This contrast is closely related to the foregoing but is not coextensive with either. It is similar to Riesman's "inner-directed — other-directed" polarity. A culture, like that of the Soviet elite, may give clear primacy to group goals and yet insist sharply on the autonomous responsibility of the individual. Traditional Russian culture, on the other hand, also favored group goals but encouraged the dependence of the individual upon the group. Dominant American culture at present makes a fetish of "individualism," though one can think of few complex cultures where individuals are in fact so sensitive to the pressures of the ephemeral standards of the peer group. "Dominant" Americans are typically "individualistic" but rarely autonomous. Similarly, cultures like Kwakiutl or Plains Indian which support flagrant egoism demand at the same time dependence upon the group. Modern French culture would fall in the self-autonomy category, but medieval Christian culture accentuated altruism and personal autonomy simultaneously. All human beings have experienced dependence as infants and children. This is one of the universal "cues" from which value selection and elaboration take off. Cultures vary in the extent to which this dependence in different forms is extended into adult life or taken as the basis for reaction-formations.

---

family, my village, my tribe, my land, or even nature in general, the entire universe. . . . I can say, "Help *me* that *my* people may live" only when the self is continuous with the other. . . .

Active-Acceptant. "Active" signifies: "human effort counts"; "something can be done." This opposition is intimately tied to the determinate-indeterminate and autonomy-dependence pairs but is, again, not coextensive. Autonomy may take the active form of self-assertion or the passive form of withdrawal. The Epicureans postulated the existence of gods but believed that they too were bound by universal laws with the working-out of which the gods themselves were powerless to interfere. The Epicurean therefore accepted his lot with serene pessimism. The Buddhist also conceives of an order of things lawfully determined but intervenes actively if only in a somewhat mechanical — and often withdrawing — way. The dichotomy is thus not strictly that between activity and acceptancy. The Spanish-Americans of New Mexico, to give another example, are acceptant but active in a "being" manner. They take Florence Kluckhohn's "subjugated-to-nature" position yet nevertheless are far from completely "passive."

Discipline-Fulfilment. Roughly, this is the "Apollonian-Dionysian" contrast. The issue is between safety and adventure, between control and expansion, between "adjustment" to the culture and internal harmony. Cultures stressing the "evil" in nature would appear likely[8] to give emphasis to discipline, yet some of these cultures do emphasize either the self-realizing or the orgiastic dimensions.

Physical - Mental. Are sensual or sensuous activities and reactions given a higher place in the hierarchy than the intellectualized? This is approximately Sheldon's "cerebrotonic" category versus his "somatotonic" and "viscerotonic" combined. This pair, once more, cuts across other pairs. Thus "discipline" may be predominantly motor or otherwise "physical" or may, on the other hand, be mainly aesthetic and intellectual.

Tense-Relaxed. Aspects of culture other than sounds exhibit

[8] But see Section 4.

these pervasive qualities which refer to the whole style of life and the general tone of all, or most, activities. One might anticipate that cultures with value-emphasis upon autonomy and discipline are more likely to be "tense," but this tendency, if it exists, is by no means an exceptionless uniformity (see Table 1). Nor does "relaxed" deny the presence of anxiety or even fairly frequent paranoid-like suspicion. The test is the degree to which tension of any kind is pervasive or is more than balanced by some sense of humor and calm easygoingness. This opposition could be called "intense-bland."

Now-Then. Cultures vary widely and importantly in their conceptions of time as an unbroken continuum or as segmented by a moving present or as homogeneous and instantaneous. But from the angle of values the most significant accent would appear to be that upon the here-and-now as opposed to either past or future. The case of emphasis upon this life as contrasted with the hereafter is merely one manifestation of the now-then opposition.

Quality-Quantity. This contrast will reflect the degree of measurement or other nonqualitative standardization found in the culture.

It will also be manifest in the extent to which the culture indicates that the natural world and human experience can be atomized. Conceptions of space and time will be largely influenced by the prevalence or absence of concepts of quantity beyond ordinal and cardinal numeration.

Unique-General. According to Northrop, this is the basic opposition between oriental cultures and those of the West, between the "undifferentiated aesthetic continuum" and "the method of logical postulation." Cultures emphasizing the individual event in all of its uniqueness are not, however, likely to be quantitative. Experience is too much of a sequence of events that may not properly be dismembered. Abstractions are either avoided or treated with great suspicion. The concrete and the literal are what count. Cultures, on the other hand, that favor the general are more interested in similarities than in differences. One sensitive index of this contrast is the tendency toward stereotyping present in the culture. In sum: discreteness and particularity contrasted with abstraction and universalism. Or: "events" versus "phenomena."

Discussion. Let me repeat: this is a system of priorities, not a set of all-or-none categories. Each member of a pair will have some representation in every culture if only in variant value-emphasis held by individuals or subgroups in the larger society. In some idea and behavior systems the secondary emphasis will be more prominent than in others. While in far the greater number of cases, cultures take a pretty definite position one way or the other, there are instances where it would be plainly false to ascribe a definite "choice." Thus the Spanish-Americans regard the evil-good pair not as "mixed" so much as "uncertain." Potentialities for human afterlife and for a divine order in the universe are religiously defined as "good." Though this variety of Catholicism does not take a fully Augustinian position on the evil in human nature, elements of this view are prominent. But the decisive fact is that as regards the outcome of any particular set of events Spanish-American culture does not stress either evil or good or some blend of the two. It simply says, in effect, "We do not know." In such cases one ought perhaps to follow the practice of linguists and call this a "zero-feature."

There are two other binary oppositions that are at a different conceptual level from the foregoing which they cut across. It makes a difference whether or not the dominant value-emphases are conscious in the sense of being frequently and easily verbalized. The explicit emphases become subject to rational consideration and criticism and are probably therefore more labile. The implicit emphases are taken for granted, almost as unchangeable conditions imposed by nature. The whole or the explicit culture is analogous to what the linguists call "parole" as contrasted with "langue" to "cultural phenotype" versus "cultural genotype." All of the assumptions and categories that are unconsciously begged in the implicit culture make up the "cultural genotype." Most of the core value-emphases in most cultures are — at any rate for the majority of the culture-carriers — "genotypic" in nature.

It would also appear to make a difference whether or not the core value-emphases exhibit a positive or a negative character. It is an induction from ordinary experience that the proportion of prescriptions and proscriptions (the "do's" and "don'ts" of every culture) may be weighted more or less heavily in one direction or the other. Value-emphases are "felt" primarily as avoidances or as seekings.

CROSS-CULTURAL STUDY OF VALUE OPPOSITIONS

I shall now test whether a small body of data confirms the implications of the logical structure of the foregoing typology of value-emphases. I shall, however, reduce the number of pairs to ten. Two previous trial runs (Kluckhohn, 1956, 1959) with these data gave identical distributions for the pairs: now-quantity (then-quality), now-general (then-unique), quality-general (quantity-unique). This suggests that these are all reducible to a single value-contrast which I shall provisionally call "general-unique." I have also eliminated the "physical-mental" pair as being logically unsatisfactory. It can mean motor-visceral versus cortical or sensuous versus esthetic-intellectual. This is equivocal, and sensuousness is often involved in immediate esthetic experience. Moreover, the ratings on this pair gave more trouble to my colleagues and myself than did those of any other. Finally, the trial runs gave indications, though not absolutely clear-cut ones, that this pair and "tense-relaxed" were manifestations of the same dimension.

The first step is to rate each of the five Southwestern cultures for the ten pairs of value-emphases. The average disagreement between my own first ratings and those made independently by the "experts" on Mormon, Homesteader,[9] Spanish-American, and Zuni was just over one category per culture, and this figure is reduced appreciably with the elimination of the troublesome "physical-mental" pair. A rating scale for the intensity of each value-emphasis would be desirable because even where competent analysts can unhesitatingly plump for the same emphasis in several different cultures they also agree that this emphasis is more intense, decisive, or pervasive in one or more of these cultures than in others. However, attempts with members of the Values Project group to make such ratings were disappointing. The high reliability on all-or-none ratings waned to about 60 per cent when intensity ratings were given. This might be corrected were the criterial attributes to be spelled out more fully and more skillfully, but for the moment I must rest with all-or-none ratings. In the following list I have made two changes from previous publications. Earlier the Spanish-American position on "good-evil" was rated as a "zero feature" and that on "individual-group" as "individual." I have reversed the latter assignment since Dr. Florence Kluckhohn says that "individual" has risen to dominance quite recently. The F. Kluckhohn-Strodtbeck investigation did not determine the three rank orders on the human nature profile. Probably "zero feature" is the best designation for the good-evil pair, but I believe that "evil" and "group" were dominant in Spanish-American culture before it was so highly acculturated by Protestant-Anglo culture — and the aim is to compare the five cultures in their historical distinctiveness.

[9] "Homestead" is the pseudonym of the Texan village.

1. *Determinate*	2. *Indeterminate*	3. *Unitary*	4. *Pluralistic*
Mormon	Homestead	Mormon	Homestead
Zuni	Spanish-	Spanish-	Navaho
Navaho	American	American	
		Zuni	
5. *Good*	6. *Evil*	7. *Group*	8. *Individual*
Mormon	Homestead	Mormon	Homestead
Zuni	Spanish-	Spanish-	Navaho[10]
	American	American	
	Navaho	Zuni	
9. *Other*	10. *Self*	11. *Dependence*	12. *Autonomy*
Mormon	Homestead	Mormon	Homestead
Spanish-	Zuni	Spanish-	
American	Navaho	American	
		Zuni	
		Navaho	
13. *Active*	14. *Acceptant*	15. *Discipline*	16. *Fulfillment*
Mormon	Spanish-	Mormon	Homestead[11]
Homestead	American	Zuni	Spanish-
Zuni			American
Navaho			Navaho
17. *Tense*	18. *Relaxed*	19. *General*	20. *Unique*
Mormon	Homestead	Mormon	Spanish-
Navaho	Spanish-	Homestead	American
	American		Zuni
	Zuni		Navaho

A central problem in value-theory is: what combinations
are likely and unlikely, possible and impossible in a value-
matrix? Comprehensive intracultural and cross-cultural results
could make possible a kind of scaling, statements as to those
value-emphases which imply or exclude others. Previously (1956,
1959), I essayed an analysis of distributions — following Bloch
(1953) — into complementary, coincident, incorporating, and
overlapping. Some of the findings I believe to have been suggestive, but in an unpublished paper Drs. A. F. C. Wallace and

[10] In the past I have characterized the Navaho pattern as "familistic
individualism." This rating means that I think that "individual" is first-
order as opposed to "family" (i.e., "group"). I admit that this rating is
difficult and arguable.

[11] There are strong variants here: disciplined-tense. Following the
linguistic analogy, these could be called "allo-values."

TABLE I

	1	2	3	4	5	6	7	8	9	10	11	12	13	14	15	16	17	18	19	20
20	N/Z	S	S/N	Z	N	S/N	S/N	Z	S	N/Z	SZ/Z		N/Z	S	N	S/Z	Z	S/N	:	:
19	W	H	W	H	W	H	W	H	W	H	W	H	W/H		W	H	W	H	:	:
18	N	H/S	S/N	H	N	H/S	S/N	H	S	H/N	S/N	H	H/N	S	N	H/S	:	:	H	S/N
17	W/Z		W	N	W	N	W	N	W	N	W/Z		W/Z		W	N	:	:	W	N
16	N	H/S	S	H/Z		HS/Z	S	H/Z	S	H/Z	S/Z	H	H/Z	S	:	:	N	H/S	H	S/Z
15	W/N		W/N		W/N		W/N		W	N	W/N		W/N		:	:	W	N	W	N
14		S	S		S	S		S		S			:	:	S		S			S
13	WZ/N	H	W/N	H/Z	W/N	H/Z	W/N	H/Z	W	HZ/Z	WZ/N	H	:	:	W/N	H/Z	W/Z	H/N	W/H	N/Z
12		H		H		H		H		H	:	:	H			H		H	H	
11	WZ/N	S	WS/N	Z	W/N	S/Z	WS/N	Z	W/S	N/Z	:	:	NZ/Z	S	W/N	S/Z	WZ/N	S/N	W	SZ/Z
10	N/Z	H	N	H/Z	N	H/Z	N	H/Z	:	:	N/Z	H	HZ/Z		N	H/Z	N	H/N	H	N/Z
9	W	S	W/S		W	S	W/S		:	:	W/S		W	S	W	S	W	S	W	S
8	N	H		H/Z		H/Z	:	:		H/Z	N	H	H/Z	S		H/Z	N	H	H	N
7	W/N	S	WS/N		W/N	S	:	:	W/S	N	WS/N		W/N		W/N	S	W	S/N	W	S/N
6	N	H/S	S	H/Z	:	:	S	H/Z	S	H/Z	S/Z	H	H/Z	S	HS/Z	N	H/S	H		S/Z
5	W/N		W/N		:	:	W/N		W	N	W/N		W/N		W/N		W	N	W	N
4	N	H	:	:		H/Z		H/Z		H/Z	N	H	H/Z			H/Z	N	H	H	N
3	W/N	S	:	:	W/N	S	WS/N		W/S	N	WS/N		W/N	S	W/N	S	W	S/N	W	S/N
2	:	:	S	H		H/S	S	H	S	H	S	H	H	S		H/S		H/S	H	S
1	:	:	W/N	Z	W/N	Z	W/N	Z	W	N/Z	WZ/N		WZ/N		W/N	Z	W/Z	Z	W	N/Z

John Atkins have justifiably criticized me for truncating my table so that only one, arbitrarily selected half of the logically combinable value-emphases were examined. Here (Table 1) I present a matrix for the ten pairs. I shall scrutinize the environments of the value-emphases in terms of an informal and partial componential analysis. I shall not examine all possible logical relationships between the various sets: contrariety, equivalence, implication, independence; mutual exclusion, identity, inclusion, overlap (Wallace and Atkins, n.d.). Rather, I shall concentrate my comments upon the notions of complementarity and implication.

I shall disregard columns and rows 12 and 14 on the ground that each of these value-emphases is assigned to only a single culture out of the five. The following remaining pairs are in complementary distribution:

> indeterminate-good (2-5)
> indeterminate-discipline (2-15)
> indeterminate-tense (2-17)
> unitary-individual (3-8)
> pluralistic-good (4-5)
> pluralistic-group (4-7)
> pluralistic-other (4-9)
> pluralistic-discipline (4-15)
> good-individual (5-8)
> good-fulfillment (5-16)
> evil-discipline (6-15)
> individual-other (8-9)
> individual-discipline (8-15)

This strikes me as a fairly satisfactory yield. It should be noted, however, that there are only two cases where a pair and its converse pair are both in complementary distribution (unitary-individual, pluralistic-group; good-fulfillment, evil-discipline). The data suggest that the following dimensions are sharp discriminators: "pluralistic," "discipline," "good," "indeterminate," "individual."

A first glance at the arrays suggests that each value-emphasis can combine with any other in more or less random fashion. Excluding 12 and 14 again, there are only three rows and columns (11, 13, 18) where there are no blank squares, and two of these three involve the two value-emphases shared by four out of the five cultures. Rows 1, 3, 6, 7, 10, 16, 18, and 20 all show nine boxes with two or more entries, and these are precisely the cases where three cultures have the same value-emphases. However, a closer scrutiny of the boxes and the marginals reveals that the proportionalities are not altogether random. Rows 2, 4, 5, 8, 9, 15, 17, 19 are all based on two cultures with the same value-stress, but the spread of joinings is from one to six. The two rows (11 and 13) where four cultures are involved yield thirteen and fifteen respectively. There do seem to be some contextual restraints and implications.

There are no instances of perfectly coincident distributions across complete rows and columns. Yet there are indications of likelihood as to what goes with what. As might be expected from the complementarities listed above, "good" and "discipline" go together with only three exceptions. This probably is contrary to "common sense" anticipation, but it must be remembered that "good" here does not refer solely to conceptions of human nature but rather to the constitution of the universe and experience in general. "Pluralistic" and "evil" have rather similar distributions, and the same may be said for the converse pair ("unitary" and "good"). "Evil" and "fulfillment" go together with four exceptions. There is a detectable but lesser similarity between "individual" and "fulfillment"; "group" and "discipline." "Individual" and "self" show a similar but by no means identical distribution. This suggests that, however inadequate the present description may be, there is somehow a valid distinction rather than one being derivable from or a special case of the other. The best discriminators for complementarity and coincidence are roughly the same except that 'indeterminate" drops out for the latter category and "fulfillment" enters prominently.

It is also worth looking at the boxes which have three entries. "Determinate" and "dependence" and "unitary-group" have perfect correspondence. The three cases in the "determinate" category are also in the "active," but the latter also includes one "indeterminate" case. All of the instances in the "unitary" class fall likewise in the "dependence" class, although this includes one additional case. The coincidences for 6-16, 7-11, 10-13, 11-13, and 20-11 are also worth mentioning.

The mapping of the various co-occurrences raises the questions: which dimensions are logically dependent and therefore associated? Which are logically independent but nevertheless associated with some consistency? The following seem plausible:

Logically Dependent	*Logically Independent*
group-discipline	good-discipline
individual-self	pluralistic-evil
determinate-active	unitary-good (?)
group-dependence	evil-fulfillment
dependence-discipline	individual-fulfillment
unitary-dependence	determinate-dependence (?)
self-active (?)	unitary-group (?)
	dependence-active
	dependence-unique

There is no instance of any two cultures failing to appear in the same box. However, the environments of the value-emphases of the five cultures vary considerably. Out of 132 boxes in which there are two or more entries the combinations of value-emphases of culture-pairs are coincident in the following order:

> Mormon-Zuni 42
> Homestead-Navaho 30
> Zuni-Navaho 20
> Spanish-Zuni 20
> Spanish-Navaho 12

Homestead-Spanish 12
Mormon-Navaho 12
Mormon-Spanish 9
Homestead-Zuni 6
Mormon-Homestead 2

The distribution is symmetrical with the number of value-emphases shared by each pair of cultures except that Mormon-Spanish and Homestead-Zuni share the same number but come up with different coincidences. The "common sense" view would doubtless assert that two variants of generalized American culture (Mormon and Texan) "ought" to be close together as "should" the two Indian cultures. The striking thing is that Mormon-Homestead have a distribution that is almost completely complementary as far as coincidences are concerned. Actually, some information from the Values Project suggests that Mormon and Homesteader value-structures are only superficially alike except for the two emphases ("active" and "general") that do derive from over-all American culture. And these join only with each other but elsewhere combine with value-emphases that are complementary between the two cultures. Zuni and Mormon, on the other hand, are "theological" cultures, and the two theologies happen to share many stresses alike as regards conceptions of nature and as regards standards for human conduct. Homestead and Navaho are linked by the contrasting emphases upon "pluralistic," "evil," "individual," and "fulfillment." It is my impression from thirty-five years of observation in the region that, in fact, Mormons and Zunis get on better together and respect each other more, while Homesteaders and Navahos have more comfortable relations than Homesteaders and Zunis.

Other observations could be made upon the cultural distributions. Homestead and Spanish tend toward complementarity in rows 2, 6, and 16. There is a lesser tendency toward complementarity between Mormon and Spanish in row 9. Spanish contrasts with Mormon-Zuni in considerable portions of rows 3 and 7.

At the end of Section 3 I suggested that there were two other binary oppositions at a different conceptual level: explicit-implicit, positive-negative. Let us quickly examine the data in these terms, though I confess that nothing definitive or particularly interesting emerges at present. I do find tendencies toward the following polarities:

Explicit	*Implicit*
Determinate: all cases	Pluralistic: both cases[12]
Indeterminate: both cases	Evil: all cases
Unitary: all cases	Group: S
Good: both cases	Individual: N
Group: M and Z	Other: S
Individual: H	Self: Z
Other: M	Dependence: all cases
Self: H	Fulfillment: H
Autonomy: H	Tense: both cases
Active: all cases	Relaxed: S and Z
Acceptant: S	Unique: all cases
Discipline: both cases	
Fulfillment: H	
General: both cases	

The cutting points for these assignments are far more vague and "intuitive" than for the value-emphases proper. The above listing — if it means anything at all — probably tells us only some things we knew already: Mormons and Zunis are conscious of the determinate and unitary emphases of their theologies; Anglo-Americans are more articulate about their values than Spanish-Americans and Indians; a pervasive value-tone such as "tense" is not ordinarily verbalized, etc. Nevertheless,

---

[12] "Implicit" does not mean, of course, that this position cannot be documented from statements by Homesteaders and Navahos. Quite the contrary. What it does mean is that participants in these two cultures do not systematically and habitually generalize this position.

on the principle that failures can also be instructive, I publish the listing.

After careful consideration I likewise find it impossible to characterize any culture significantly in terms of over-all toning toward "positive" or "negative," "seeking" or "avoidance." In spite of its emphasis upon "discipline" and "tense," Mormon culture does seem dominantly toned toward "seeking." Homesteader and Zuni (despite many ritual prohibitions) value-stress appears mainly positive. Spanish is more mixed but leaning in the positive direction. Although Navaho culture is "determinate" and "active," it is the best case for negative value-toning.

This is the end, for the moment, of this small exploration. I would argue only that schemas of this general order need to be further worked out theoretically and tried out empirically with many assemblages of data if cross-cultural comparison of values is to become comprehensive, parsimonious, and fruitful. I believe that a more formal and rigorous use of componential analysis will then become possible and will be the most likely avenue for attaining conceptual equivalences across cultural boundaries. And this is essential if we are to move beyond the empirical *description* of values.

*William L. Kolb is Professor and head of the
Department of Sociology and Anthropology,
Carleton College; president of the Southwestern
Sociological Society, 1950; head of the Department of
Sociology and Anthropology, Newcomb College, Tulane
University, 1948-1959; presently member of the Executive
Committee and also the Council of the American Sociological
Association; writing and research interests in the theory
of values, sociology of religion and systematic theory;
authored* Sociological Analysis *(with Logan Wilson),
1949, and many other publications.*

William L. Kolb

VALUES, DETERMINISM AND ABSTRACTION

IT IS EXTREMELY DIFFICULT TO DISCUSS A PAPER OF THE SORT Professor Kluckhohn has presented. Unlike a short research paper or theoretical note, the present work is concerned with several themes and problems, and these in turn are deeply rooted in Professor Kluckhohn's long-standing concern for the entire field of values as an area of social science investigation. My selection of aspects of the paper for discussion and my manner of treating them, in turn, can only be understood in light of my own concern for the scientific study of values.

Let me say at once that I share Professor Kluckhohn's belief that values, as aspects of human action and culture, consisting of standards of selection, explicitly embodied in symbols or implicitly present in modes of selective orientation which transcend immediate desire, are empirical phenomena susceptible to observation and analysis. Further, I believe that any statements about values which are to have the status of sociological or anthropological propositions must be subject to the same tests of empirical verification as any other scientific proposition. These shared beliefs are rooted in certain nonempirically demonstrable presuppositions concerning the nature, the importance, and the possibility of knowing that realm which we call empirical reality. I believe that Professor Kluckhohn and I share these presuppositions.

There are, however, certain other presuppositions, usually

taken for granted in contemporary social science and manifested, I believe, in Professor Kluckhohn's paper, that I do not share. I do not think these presuppositions are necessary for an empirically oriented social science; and I do think that they render impossible a scientific study of values adequate to their full empirical reality. I refer to the presuppositions of determinism and maximum abstraction. The first of these presuppositions is reflected most clearly in the account of Florence Kluckhohn's and Fred Strodtbeck's study; and the second in the approach to value-system comparison outlined in the latter part of the paper.

THE QUESTION OF DETERMINISM

Professor Kluckhohn's statement concerning the Kluckhohn-Strodtbeck study which I find most important in the present context is the following:

> But — and this is the new point — basic value shifts occur when external pressures impinge upon the already existent variation in the system. The systematic variation always contains the potentiality for change but remains dormant or latent until environmental events or intensified contacts with other cultures bring a second — or third — order position into dominance. If this be correct, we escape the puzzling *mystique* of "immanent causation." My wife had studied the values of the Spanish-American village fifteen years before the field work of the Values Project was carried out. At that time the lineal orientation was definitely dominant. By 1951 it had become, by a shade, subordinate to the individualistic orientation. This shift she had predicted in 1936 and specified the variant individuals who would be the bearers of the trend.

Now I am not concerned about the fact that the values changed under the impact of changed conditions, nor am I concerned about the fact that the changes were predicted. It would be strange indeed if changing circumstances did not have an impact on values; and prediction in human affairs can be made both on the basis of knowledge of determined linkages, internal and external, and upon the basis of emphatic introspection or *verstehen* which is both a method of hypothesizing internal determined linkages and of discerning motives and probable free choice. Freedom is only potentially unpredictable in all cases; in many cases it can be successfully predicted.

I am concerned about the way in which the relationship between value-change and environmental change seems to be conceived and about the reference to "immanent causation," if I interpret it correctly. I am not denying external change as a causal factor of changes in value-system, but I do believe that there are several sources of immanent change in values which in no sense involve a mystique and I also do not believe that external change, even when it occurs, is the sole determinant of change, nor that the change is totally determined by any combination of variables.

First, with respect to immanent change, is not each of us aware that he could if he would change his ultimate commitments? At least this awareness — true or false — is an empirical fact, and if we accept its truth as a matter of keeping our sanity, then we must accept that to which it refers as a source of immanent change. Although this freedom of each of us is available to the direct experience of each one of us alone, this is not to claim that it is unmotivated. But there are immanent motivations and unchanging external pressures, as well as changing ones. All value-systems — I suggest — are inherently unstable because they are never totally adequate to certain universal and unchanging aspects of the human condition, first because they are finite, and second, because they are always *partly* rationalizations and projections rather than ultimate convictions. There is always the possibility that the pressure of the human condition which in its meaning-questioning elements is fundamentally unchanging may motivate change in the value-system, which would appear to be immanent; internally there must always be pressure for change unless man rationalizes his finiteness and rationalizations into an assumption of pure conviction and absolute knowledge. Finally it can be said almost with certainty that every elite will move in on its own value-system and every non-elite will rationalize its interests as well. All this is not to say that external change cannot produce its own pressure; it is to deny that immanent causality is a "mystique."

Even when we see the causal efficacy of "environmental" factors, there remains the crucial problem of the way in which these factors are seen to be related to the value-system and the human self. The point of view which I accept and which seems to me to be missing in the passage cited is stated as follows by Parsons in his discussion of Max Weber:

> As a generalized result of these studies, he found that it was not possible to reduce the striking variation of pattern on the level of religious ideas in these cases to any features of an independently existent social structure or economic situation, though he continually insisted on the very great importance of situational factors in a number of different connections. These factors, however, served only to pose the problems with which great movements of religious thought have been concerned. But the distinctive cognitive patterns were only understandable as a result of a cumulative tradition of intellectual effort in grappling with the problems thus presented and formulated.[1]

This position requires the presupposition of human freedom, for as B. F. Skinner has pointed out, if determinism is presupposed, internal psychological categories — such as intellectual grappling — may be convenient logical linkages or intervening variables and may even be "real"; but for purposes of prediction and control, responses *are* reducible to the impact of external variables.[2] If values are to be considered more than epipheno-

---

[1] Talcott Parsons (1949), p. 62.
[2] B. F. Skinner (1953), pp. 23-42.

mena or more than independent variables in the sense that within a restricted context they may be regarded as causally related to patterns of behavior, they must be seen empirically as resting on the ultimate commitments which men freely make in the face of the human condition. They are conditioned by psychological needs, external conditions, constant and changing, and by self- and group-centered interests, but they are not and cannot be regarded as totally determined.

And again I would like to stress that by freedom I do not mean simply the opposite of determinism in the sense of contingency, or caprice. Freedom must appear in scientific analysis primarily as potential or actual unpredictability, and as a constant conceptual reminder that we do choose and are responsible. But like conditioning in the classical sense it is a presupposition which when examined is not empirically demonstrable in itself, but can be shown empirically to exist as an element of the experience of each of us. And in that experience each of us knows that while it is not determinism, neither is it chance, but rather responsible choice. It will not do to leave this concept out of our scientific description and analysis of values on the argument that science deals with values only insofar as they are determined. Certainly it is our task to deal with the whole range of human experience, or at least to relate one part of it to another; if we do not do this deliberately, we do it undeliberately by coming to identify our deterministic image of man with the whole of concrete empirical reality and by attempting to ground our faith and our policy in such an image.

THE ADEQUACY OF MAXIMUM ABSTRACTION

The second aspect of Professor Kluckhohn's paper which I wish to examine briefly is his discussion of the thirteen dichotomies in terms of which he wishes to compare variations in value-systems. There are several ways in which this might be approached. It would be possible, for example, to examine and criticize each of the pairs. From my own point of view the split between determinism and freedom is much more significant than the dichotomy between lawfulness and chance; and as I have indicated, I object strongly to lumping chance and freedom together. Or it would be possible to examine the logic by which this particular system of classification is regarded as exhaustive of the universally significant foci of value-choice. I am appalled at the number of systems of classification of values, pattern variables, and value-orientations that are running loose today, each claiming, so far as I can see, to be exhaustive at the same or similar level of abstraction; and each failing to give a full-scale logical ground for its claim. There is an over-all rationale for classification as such and a need for justification for certain categories of classification in particular, both of which must be carefully thought out if the present trend in social theory is to continue.

Yet, fundamentally, these problems do not disturb me so much as does the assumption of the desirability of the maximum level of abstraction which lies behind the present effort at comparison as well as most of the other systems of classification of values. It is true to say as Professor Kluckhohn has said that "In some way we must attain conceptual equivalence across cultural boundaries if more than the scientific *description* of values is to become possible." But it does not follow that classification at an almost contentless level of abstraction is the proper manner of establishing conceptual equivalence. Classification, although always aiming at real identities, is always concerned with identities for the purposes at hand. What are the purposes of comparing value-systems, and what level of abstraction can best serve this purpose?

One thing that is frequently forgotten about scientific abstraction is that the elements logically abstracted empirically remain as parts of the web of phenomena; and the abstraction is important only if in some way it facilitates the understanding and prediction of the relations of these elements in their concrete manifestations. It is legitimate to abstract "rationality," for example, only if one can, through the method of successive approximations, come back to the manner in which rationality empirically combines with other empirical elements to issue into courses of concrete action. In the natural sciences the conceptual schemes do finally grasp physical phenomena empirically, and the modes of classification are capable of grasping all of the significant empirical elements.

In the human sciences while such highly formal categories as status, role, institution, and value-system do permit the conceptualizing of social relations in general, what are essentially content concepts are not so easily generalized. The number, the complexity, the modes of variation of the variables of human action at the historical level of empirical reality in which we are interested in them does not permit — at least at this time — a mode of classification at a level of abstraction which permits definitive comparison of value-systems in all significant aspects on the one hand and relevant historical comparison and analysis of value-systems on the other.

This is not to say that general categories for purposes of value-comparison cannot be used, but these categories must exist at a relatively low level of abstraction, clinging close to the level of history, and they must permit a point by point comparison relevant to historical analysis for certain purposes. Thus Max Weber's famous comparison of exemplary prophetism, immanentism, other-worldly mysticism with ethical prophetism, transcendentalism, and worldly asceticism was not meant to apply to all value-systems indiscriminately nor, to the value-systems he selected, for all purposes. Protestantism, Catholicism, Judaism, and the Eastern religions were compared, not in general, but in terms of elements that were relevant to a certain kind of economic order. While the categories used were general, they were not part of a total system of concepts for classifying all value-systems, to say nothing of all societies, or even for classifying Protestantism, Catholicism, Judaism, and the Eastern religions in *all* their significant characteristics or for the purpose of understanding their relations to *all* other social variables.

One may, indeed one must, hope that ultimately ways of developing more inclusive patterns of generalization and comparison of value-systems will be found. Indeed the formal categories of social system analysis have already broadened the scope of such comparison. But in the meantime the problem of the historicity of human action, at the level at which we are really interested in it, remains; and I believe that there exist in the categories of disciplines, such as philosophy and theology today, concepts at a level of concreteness and specificity more adequate to the kinds of comparison of value-systems we want and need to make, than those which are found in the present efforts at abstraction in sociology and anthropology.

3

Values and Education
in America

Robin M. Williams, Jr. has been Professor of Sociology at Cornell University since 1946 and chairman of the department since 1956; director of the Social Science Research Center, 1949-1954; president of the American Sociological Society, 1958; has held various research positions with governmental agencies, e.g. in the War Department, 1942-1945; among his many publications: The Reduction of Intergroup Tensions, *1947;* The American Soldier, *vols. I and II (with others);* American Society, *1951 (revised 1960); and* Schools in Transition, *1954; an active member of many professional associations and consultant to governmental and non-governmental organizations.*

Robin M. Williams, Jr.

VALUES AND MODERN EDUCATION IN THE UNITED STATES

INTRODUCTION

WE MUST BEGIN BY DEALING BRIEFLY WITH CERTAIN DEFINITIONS and assumptions which will be found useful in talking about our subject. Our mandate is to analyze "values" in "education." What meaning shall we attach to these terms?

This is not the place to review the enormous body of technical literature which treats of the concept "value" and of related notions such as belief, attitude, opinion, ideology. Nor, even if our competence permitted, could we here take the time to deal with the many important philosophical questions raised by the conception, value. At the very least, however, it is necessary to state a few crucial distinctions.

There seems to be rather widespread agreement that in the consideration of values a useful point of departure lies in the brute facts of *preference* and *selection*. Men prefer some things to others; they select particular objects and courses of action out of a range of objective possibilities present in a situation. At least some human social behavior is purposive, in the sense that people can and do state their goals in advance and then be observed to act as if they were in fact pursuing those ends. Objects, events, experiences are desired and sought out, or are eschewed or avoided. Man is not a creature of indifference; the world is not emotionally neutral for him, nor are all things equally desired or esteemed; pushpin is not as good as poetry for most of us, most of the time. Upon reflection, however, it has become evident that a highly consequential distinction must be drawn early in the game between "value" in the sense of an *evaluation of* an object of regard, on the one hand, and the *standards* upon which such evaluations are predicted. We find it natural to say such things as, "Americans place a high value upon education," "that certainly was a worthwhile experience," "he is a most valuable member of our organization," or "political democracy is the best form of government." These are evaluations *of* objects, as when it is said: "The value placed upon 'future success' has receded in favor of 'respectable and stable security' seen in shorter time range."[1] It is precisely to the fact of placing a value *on* something to which we often are referring in ordinary speech when we use the term "value." On the other hand, we frequently find ourselves using the same word to refer to the standards by which evaluations are made and in terms of which choices and evaluations are defended and justified, to ourselves and others. Although Professor Kluckhohn now modestly deprecates his own earlier definition, we are indebted to his work for a clear formulation of the distinction between "that which is desired" and "that which is desirable" (worthy of being desired, properly the object of desire, etc.). Values in the sense of standards are "conceptions of the desirable." What these standards are is not immediately given to us by knowing the goals men seek, the ideologies they profess, or the gross preferences they exhibit in their conduct.[2] To know that a man seeks, say, money or success, tells us next to nothing about the *criteria* in terms of which these goals are judged worthwhile.

Later on we shall have occasion to examine educational aims

---

[1] Clyde Kluckhohn, in Elting E. Morrison (1958), p. 204.
[2] It is clear also from the foregoing that values are not identical with "motives" or "needs" of individual personalities.

and goals. Our primary interest will be not in the particular aims and ideologies but rather in what we can infer as to underlying criteria of goodness and appropriateness. For present purposes, in short, values are criteria or standards. We want to know what standards of desirability are employed by educators, students, and indeed, the public at large, in evaluating education, in setting educational goals, in choosing methods of instruction, in selecting students and teachers, and so on.

We are using the term education in a very simple common-sense way to refer to what goes on in the ordinary processes of our elementary and secondary schools and colleges and universities. Looked at in one way, of course, all of life is education, but this view is too broad to be very useful. We must draw a line somewhere. While recognizing the enormous total impact of the mass media, of in-service and on-the-job training in business, government and elsewhere, and, indeed, of training in the family, we shall deal primarily with formal education in the specialized and organizationally separate forms so familiar to us in the current American scene.

Before getting into the main matter at hand, it may be valuable to quickly glance at the relation between values and science (and scholarly work more generally). A short generation ago it apparently was believed by many educators and scientists that scientific activity could be wholly isolated from the realm of values; "science" inhabited a world of neutral facts, in which, undeterred by questions of value, it pursued empirical knowledge by objective methods. Its truths were subject to intersubjective confirmation, regardless of their value-implications.

With the benefit of hindsight and further thought, we can now see that these matters are not quite so simple as they once may have seemed to be. Without questioning the objective character of the impressive accumulation of scientific knowledge, we are nevertheless nowadays more clearly aware of the inevitable "relevance of values" in all inquiry. Values enter into the choice of problems for study — whether attention is to be directed to the mechanism of a spider's knee, nuclear fission, metaphor in Wordsworth, leadership in small groups, endocrine functions, maze-learning among white rats, international trade balances, or what. And surely no one any longer demands to be convinced that the results of scientific work are highly consequential in terms of values. "Science" itself represents a definite value-position: it has its own final virtues and its special norms. Its mode of treating with the world is not the same as that of art, religion, or philosophy, and clarity is not advanced by pretending otherwise.

And the case of science is a special case of the place of value in education more generally. To educate at all is to educate for something. If one does not intend to *change* the student, why bother to teach at all? At the very least, one intends to open up doors and windows, to help the student discover for himself some of his potentialities for doing, thinking, feeling, valuing. How we will educate depends both upon our values and upon our knowledge and our ideas concerning reality.

An example may be in order. The idea that thinking is socially conditioned, even to the extent of determining the criteria of truth, has already profoundly affected educational policy and practice in the higher levels. The combined impact of an impressive list of 19th- and 20th-century thinkers — one need only recall such names as Marx, Freud, Sorel, Veblen, Mannheim — has persuasively set forth the case for believing that existential social conditions "determine" ideas, that reality varies with the perspectives of the beholder. This momentous contention easily leads to a kind of relativism which, although it definitely does *not* logically follow from the thesis properly understood,[3]

---

[3] Charles Frankel (1959), p. 133. "The simple point is that all thinking has its physical, psychic, and social determinants; but this in no way implies that human beings cannot be objective."

would seem to have a peculiar affinity with a pluralistic culture, marked by pragmatic emphases, many instrumentally-oriented human relationships, much social mobility, economic and political manipulation, and a considerable amount of *anomie*. Disillusion, distrust, alienation, apathy, and the like — to the extent that they are generated in this situation — furnish fertile ground for the growth of an *intellectual* uncertainty that can then contribute further to amorphous ethics, nonprincipled "tolerance," political apathy, and generalized cynicism.

I see no compelling reason for failing to state that I do not regard as desirable the consequences just hypothesized. The present task, however, is not that of evaluation but of attempting to understand the significance of values in education under circumstances of this kind.

The first crucial essential in this attempt is to see that the choice is not merely that of educational drift versus organized indoctrination of values. Let us note that education which is anything more than simple instruction in skills or in elementary concepts and procedures has always had to deal with the problem of ordering and stabilizing what would otherwise be dim, vague, shifting, chaotic, and ambiguous in our thoughts and feelings. Of course, no one could believe that the search for clarity and order has been the only aim or even always a major aim, of education. But surely it is a fact that such a quest is a genuine component of anything we could properly call education. History preserves and organizes memories. Instruction and criticism in arts and letters help to clarify and organize preferences, to evoke new sensitivities, to maintain and create canons of taste. The physical sciences can, at their best, both unfold a vision of order in nature and provide a remarkable set of rules and procedures for discerning that order. The social sciences can, at their best, offer the student still another image of orderliness, often not hitherto suspected, behind the appearance of complexity and flux in the world of human conduct.

I am thinking here of matters that have been so well expressed by Professor Frankel that I can do no better than to quote his remarks at some length. He says:

> If we take the modern university as an example, 'the speculative faculties' of man engage in three principal types of enterprise. There is, first, the sort of research and teaching that concerns itself with objects that arrest the mind or delight the eye or ear, with experiences that exercise the emotions, and the symbols that express human ideals and aspirations. Secondly, there is a type of activity that has to do with keeping the memory of the past alert and alive. Finally, there is a sort of activity which attempts to organize and explain events by general principles. The first of these may be called 'criticism,' the second 'history,' and the third 'science.' But while these are now highly organized, professional activities, they come into the world with a natural pedigree and a practical vocation. They are the ordinary concerns of a creature whose energies are not natively in balance with the world he inhabits, who is not brute enough to proceed on instinct alone and not divine enough to see or do all things at once.[4]

To repeat, our first conclusion is that the activity of educating represents preference, choice, hence evaluation. What is taught is not just an automatic reflection of an objective world — "objective" in the sense that no preferences are involved and no criteria of selection applied. Education cannot avoid dealing with values, either in the case of evaluations of the world or in the case of the standards in terms of which judgments of desirability are made. In those instances in which education really does its job, it gives hands and feet to feelings and values. It provides conceptual structure, defining and stabilizing the criteria for value-judgments and for the selection of objects of choice.

Furthermore, everything we know about personalities and

[4] *Ibid.*, p. 148.

social systems is consistent with the prediction that education in any particular society will always manifest, in some degree, the value-patterns prevailing in the larger system of which education is a partially autonomous part.

AMERICAN INSTITUTIONS AND VALUE-SYSTEMS IN RELATION TO EDUCATION

Obviously, educational aims vary from one society to another and from one historical period to another within the same society, and these aims are always related to the other institutions and basic value-orientations prevailing in the society or community under examination. On net balance it seems reasonable to agree with Orville Brim's contention that on the whole " . . . the educational system of a society is the means whereby traditional culture is preserved, and that any new values it transmits within one generation are fractional compared to the massive tradition it imparts."[5] In the United States, for a long time now, a chorus of voices has told us that this is a rapidly changing society. This belief in rapid change has become almost a point of national pride, and it may verge upon being unpatriotic to question this article of faith too closely. Yet it is easy to exaggerate the extent of really basic change, especially in values rather than just in the specific institutional arrangements in which values are expressed and implemented. The America of 1959 is not that of 1859, and certainly not that of 1776. But there are common elements in all periods, and a definite and recognizable continuity in the course of development of the society. Some of the basic values and conceptions of the nature of man held at the birth of the Republic are still widespread and viable. No one of us expects the America of 25 or 50 years hence to be the same as that of today, but we would be surprised, and rightly so, were it not to bear a definite family resemblance to our present society. Not only change, but

[5] Orville G. Brim, Jr. (1958), pp. 16-17.

also continuity and even stability are part of the reality of American life. And our educational institutions affect, as well as being affected by, the shifting balance of forces making for change or stability in the environing society and culture.

At the risk of oversimplification and possibly of unwitting distortion, let us try to make explicit a few of the major characteristics of our institutions and value-systems that seem most relevant to education today. America is, to use the well-worn phrase once more, a pluralistic society. Things often repeated may come to be accepted without the attention they actually merit. Perhaps this is true of the theme of unity and diversity in American society. So often have we been told that here is the example par excellence of a pluralistic society, of a unique "laboratory of intergroup relations," of an orchestration of cultural differences, of the unity of political and economic interdependence. From most of the major societies, although of course predominantly from European countries, have come the representatives of diverse cultures who were the forefathers of "that new man, the American." A nation of nations, a multiple melting pot, a cultural medley — so run the suggestive phrases. There is the diversity of ethnic and "racial" categories, of religious affiliations, of regions and localities, of rural and urban areas, of socio-economic classes, of thousands of specialized occupations and hundreds of occupational subcultures. Underneath much overt uniformity, substantial diversity continues to exist in this industrialized and urbanized society. With rapid technological advance and a highly developed industrial and commercial system, it experiences a high level of material prosperity. Self-subsistent local economies have almost completely disappeared. A seamless web of economic interdependence links every part of the country with every other and connects the American economy with an international system of trade. Complex large-scale organizations abound. Mass communication is all-pervasive. Increased reliance upon centralized political authority, already favored by other basic forces, is accentuated by the responsibilities and hazards of a leading world power in an unforseeably long period of international tension. The inherited political and administrative forms and arrangements are strained, tested, and reshaped by unprecedented pressures and requirements. An open-class system, coupled with widespread economic opportunity and high rates of geographic mobility, result in extensive mixing and intermingling of people of diverse origins and backgrounds. Partly by virtue of the same causes, we have developed an extraordinarily stripped-down kinship system, involving new definitions of the family unit and of the roles of men and women, parents and children.

It is a sociological cliché, but no less true for all that, to say that such a system involves individuals in a multiplicity of segregated roles, exposes them to different views of life and specific standards of conduct, creates frequent shifts in personal relationships and group affiliations.

In a culture which strongly emphasizes universalistic rules and an active, instrumental approach to life, the stress upon individual achievement, especially in business occupations, tends to direct attention and energy away from collective goals, as well as away from expressive and contemplative concerns. Although these emphases may be changing, they are still strong enough to lend a distinctive quality to this innovative, flexible, open-ended system.

In an earlier investigation, I tried to broadly characterize dominant value-themes in American society in the following terms:

1)   American culture is organized around the attempt at *active mastery* rather than *passive acceptance*. Into this dimension fall the low tolerance of frustration; the refusal to accept ascetic renunciation; the positive encouragement of desire; the stress on power; the approval of ego-assertion, and so on.

2)   It tends to be interested in the *external world* of things

and events, of the palpable and immediate, rather than in the inner experience of meaning and affect. Its genius is manipulative rather than contemplative.

3)   Its world-view tends to be *open* rather than closed: it emphasizes change, flux, movement; its central personality types are adaptive, accessible, outgoing and assimilative.

4)   In wide historical and comparative perspective, the culture places its primary faith in *rationalism* as opposed to *traditionalism;* it de-emphasizes the past, orients strongly to the future, does not accept things just because they have been done before.

5)   Closely related to the above, is the dimension of *orderliness* rather than unsystematic *ad hoc* acceptance of transitory experience. (This emphasis is most marked in the urban middle classes.)

6)   With conspicuous deviations, a main theme is a *universalistic* rather than a *particularistic* ethic.

7)   In interpersonal relations, the weight of the value-system is on the side of "horizontal" rather than "vertical" emphases: peer-relations, not superordinate-subordinate relations; equality rather than hierarchy.

8)   Subject to increased strains and modifications, the received culture emphasizes *individual personality* rather than group identity and responsibility.

Although naturally selective and incomplete, this formulation still seems to be valid, at a very general level, and to be suggestive of important questions concerning American education.

Assuming that the above brief sketch of salient social and cultural characteristics is not essentially inaccurate, if we knew nothing whatever about the actual character of American education, we would still be able to guess that in such a sociocultural setting it would be likely to have certain predictable characteristics. We would expect it to be specialized, institutionally segregated, highly organized. We would not be surprised to find a mass-education system, emphasizing equality of opportunity and attuned to vocational preparation. We would expect educational activities to reflect a search for unity-in-diversity. We might even guess that the total educational enterprise might reveal a diversity of aims, the presence of conflicting values and cross-purposes, and a considerable amount of uncertainty and ambivalence concerning goals and methods.

Of course we cannot make these "predictions," because we know too much about the answers before we ask the questions. We do have mass education. A high-school education is coming to be thought of as essential and taken-for-granted by rapidly increasing numbers; a college degree, once the rare privilege of a small elite, is on the way of being conceived as practically a democratic right. The system emphasizes equality of opportunity, no matter how imperfectly the desideratum may be realized in some cases. The educational system is highly responsive to public demands and pressures, local, state, and national. Educational offerings are highly varied; practicality and individual competition and success are objects of high regard.

For understanding education in society of the kind being examined here, it is important to point out that education has economic "value." It may be less trite to point this out if we refer, not to the *individual's* enhanced earning power acquired through education for competitive placement in the occupational system, but rather to the "multiplier effect" of education upon the productive power of an economy. To Peter Drucker we owe the aphorism: "Education is now one basic capital resource . . . the real capital of a developed country is education. . . "[6] In a way the educated person is an elaborately transformed resource of nature; were a person a machine — which happily, of course, is not the case — the inherent properties he has of being in such large measure self-starting, self-propelled,

---

[6] Peter F. Drucker, in R. Wayne Kernodle (1959), p. 58.

self-repairing, ingenious, flexible, self-directing, problem-solving, equipped with enormous memory-banks — such qualities would impress any engineer or economist as great assets for increasing the real wealth of any economic system. Without elaborating the argument, it seems plain enough that education is, in one of its protean guises, a process of capital-formation. Nor is it merely a fanciful analogy, I think, to conceive of verified knowledge, transmitted or circulated through educational processes, as a sort of social money, reliably exchangeable in kind, and redeemable in other "goods" as well.

It is commonplace to note that formal education in America, once it shed its earlier religious and classical cast, has been notably pragmatic and vocationally-oriented. In spite of recent concern with "general education" and "education for citizenship," these emphases remain prominent. Present "runaway" needs for technicians, engineers, scientists, and mathematicians seem likely, on the whole, to increase the emphasis upon applied, vocational objectives. The urgent demands of industry and military agencies for highly trained specialists will not be easy to resist, and many educators certainly will not wish to resist them.

Throughout our history, however, and continuing today, a vocal minority has opposed the relegation of humanities and theoretic science to a secondary place in the instructional system. Sometimes the voices raise sharp questions: "Perhaps, in a mass society, the school cannot be the transmitter of civilized values but only a complex of training programs for various skill groups?"[7] The ideal of the mind broadly trained to understand and appreciate the whole of life is not likely to disappear, but we have the impression that it is not likely soon to win a dominant place.

Truly speculative thought has never had a place of high

[7] Philip Rieff (1957), p. 233.

honor with us, save in theology and in the case of a very few philosophers and political thinkers, and then within limited circles. The same can be said for basic theoretic work in the sciences. Perhaps the persisting cultural emphasis upon specialized occupational preparation has something to do with the oft-deplored fact that in many fields we still have to import most of the really important theoretic developments from Europe. It may well be, however, that this situation is already on its way to a basic transformation. No less informed an observer than J. Robert Oppenheimer recently said: "Today in almost all fields of natural science, and in some others as well, our country is as pre-eminent in theory as it is in experiment, invention, and practice."[8]

However, one can only agree with such British writers as Laski and Brogan that American education is likely to be greatly misunderstood if it is viewed solely as a means of advancing and transmitting knowledge. Certainly it does create and disseminate knowledge. However, another central function of the public schools and nonsectarian universities is the teaching of young people from diverse backgrounds in a set of common ideas and social standards. They teach "Americanism," perhaps more effectively by unwitting precept and example than by drill in creeds and forms. Our educational system is one of the great agencies of all time for inducing voluntary consensus and conformity. More will be said of this later.

DILEMMAS AND CONFLICTS OF VALUES

In a very literal sense it seems fair to say that "American education" has no overarching, clear, unitary, and definite agenda of value-priorities. Certainly, as indeed we have just argued, pervasive and marked commonalities of value can

---

[8] J. Robert Oppenheimer, in Elting E. Morrison (1958), pp. 116-117. Immediately he adds: "But there is no unifying theory of what human life is about."

be discerned across wide sectors of our educational undertakings. But the actual diversity, compromises, and eclecticism are too apparent to permit one to formulate an inclusive "philosophy" or a single value-creed which could be said to unify the whole into one coherent program. Shall we seek to produce "scholars" or "workers" or "gentlemen"?[9] Or, if all three, in what numbers, proportions, and order — and how? What is our conception of the Good Man who is to emerge from the educational process — the religious man, the patriot or nativist, the man of the market, the Common Man, or the humanist?[10] Do we wish to give everyone all the formal education he can absorb, at the risk of dragging down the more gifted to the pace and level of the lowest common denominator? Do we wish to give maximum emphasis to the special training of a highly selected group of the most able, at the risk of inequality of opportunity and the development of a gap between "elite" and "mass"?

Even more broadly, how much do Americans really "place a high value on" education? It is a widely publicized fact that the real income of teachers has decreased in a period when most other occupational groups were enjoying increased purchasing power, that the average "intelligence" scores of college graduates and graduate students entering teaching are below the average for all professions, that elementary and secondary public teachers are preponderantly lower middle-class women. What do these facts tell us about the actual evaluation of education in our society?

To return to the basic question earlier posed. In what conceivable ways do values show themselves in education? We would suggest the following primary modes:

1)   In the choice of educational aims,

    (a)   the specific content to be taught
    (b)   the model of the educated person to be sought.

[9] Malcolm S. Maclean (1938).
[10] H. Otto Dahlke (1958).

In a structurally complicated society with many highly specialized and skilled trades and professions, the range of specific
education content required even for vocational preparation
alone is very wide, and a rich and diverse cultural heritage
vastly extends the total scope of desired curricula. The founder
of my home university is credited (or blamed) with having
said, "I would found an institution in which any person can
find instruction in any subject." Were Ezra Cornell to return
today to the university which bears his name, he might be
amazed at how completely his expressed intention has been realized. If there is such a thing as a characteristic American style
in the choice of curricula, methods, and the end-products to
be sought in education, perhaps it is a tendency to avoid ultimate choices of values by trying to provide something for
every point of view. Yet to let this statement stand by itself
would be misleading and unfair. For specific schools and colleges and universities do sometimes make decisive choices of
emphasis — to give high-quality liberal education, to impart
superior professional training, to produce good citizens, or well-
adjusted personalities, or religiously devout and competent
leaders. The total effect of the numerous diverse educational organizations, however, is to represent nearly every conceivable educational aim and value-criterion to be found in the larger society.

2)   In the choice of students to be exposed to educational
efforts. The major dilemma here seems to be one to which earlier
reference has been made: the "Jacksonian" effort to extend
education as widely as possible versus the "Jeffersonian" ideal
of highly developed training of a relatively small, select con-
tingent of the most highly qualified. In our present prosperous
and easygoing situation, we undoubtedly will try to have our
cake and eat it too. But there may come a time when we will
need to choose how to evaluate excellence of intellectual attainment as over against competing standards of selection and
competing goals.

3)   In the provision or lack of provision for the supportive, custodial, disciplinary, protective, caretaking, therapeutic, and other social-emotional aspects of the realistic situation of students in contexts of exposure to instruction.

At what level, if any, and to what extent are we prepared to put the student "on his own" in these matters? The extraordinary amount of supportive and custodial effort manifest in our colleges and universities undoubtedly reflects humane values, concern for the worth of individual personality, "puritan" traditions, and a variety of other considerations. Do the measures all take actually serve the values we intend them to support? How far do we go in protecting students against failure or, in general, against the consequences of autonomous behavior? And with what *other* consequences?

4)   In the effective definition of the roles of teachers, students, administrators, and other social types involved in the total educational enterprise. There are numerous polarities in this area: authority-freedom, conformity-independence, the lone scholar versus the 'team," the "community of scholars" versus bureaucratic modes of organization. It appears that there often exists an enormous cognitive gap between our explicit values and the institutional forms within which we seek to operate.

5)   In the emphasis given to the creation of knowledge (in the broadest sense), as over against the transmission of knowledge. It must be a very rare seat of higher learning in this country in which there is not tension and conflict centering upon this persistent dilemma. It appears in the support given to research versus teaching. Its resolution in differing ways leads to widely different educational styles in different units and levels of the system.

6)   In choosing the methods and basic orientations concerned with the development of "personality" and "character." There are the goals of psychological harmony, adjustment, clari-

ty, autonomy, inner integrity. These psychiatric desiderata are often in conflict with the organizational demands for rigidly scheduled modes of adaptation, the psychological needs for security, reassuring obedience, and rigid standards on the part of teachers and educational administrators, and the value-orientations of both competitive occupational life and bureaucratic conformism.[11] There are kinds of teaching and learning that exact heavy psychological costs. And there are modes of educating for personal adjustment and group adaptation that seem to involve severe sacrifices in individuality and creativity and intellectual clarity and penetration. We are currently hearing much criticism of the alleged costs of educational practices which are aimed at producing smooth adjustment to group living. The value-issues are often not clearly confronted, and a creative synthesis of the clashing demands is not yet widely apparent.

7) In deciding, in specific situations and with reference to other value-considerations, whether and to what extent and how education is to be "secular" or "religious" and in the evaluating what this very complex distinction may signify.

8) In itself providing a valuable inner resource for the consumer. For certainly one of the "conceptions of the desirable" which we find running through educational processes is that of aiding the individual to unfold his potentialities, to extend the scope and acuteness of his experience, to more clearly and richly know the external world, other people, and himself.

These modalities of value-involvement in education are assuredly not exhaustive of the actual possibilities. But they may serve to illustrate the pervasiveness and complexity of considerations of value in the area of our present interest; compromises, restless re-examination, and continuing dialogue and debate characterize the present educational scene.

[11] Dana L. Farnsworth (1955), pp. 95-104.

VALUES OF AMERICAN COLLEGE STUDENTS

But it would not be very satisfactory to leave our conclusions at the point just reached. Fortunately, it is possible to be somewhat more concrete and factual in diagnosing the involvement of values in education. For this purpose we now draw upon data from sociological and psychological studies of students in American colleges and universities, and particularly from the Cornell Values Studies. In the latter research program, information is available for 2,758 Cornell students surveyed in 1950 and for 1,571 students surveyed in 1952. Of the latter sample, 944 persons had been studied two years earlier; hence *changes* in attitudes and values can be analyzed for identical individuals at two points in time. In addition, the 1952 study collected comparable data from 4,585 students at ten other colleges and universities scattered across the country: Dartmouth, Harvard, Yale, Wesleyan, North Carolina, Fisk, Texas, University of California at Los Angeles, Wayne, and Michigan.

We find, in the first place, that *the students overwhelmingly approve of higher education,* positively evaluate the job their own institution is doing, do not accept most of the criticisms levelled against higher education in the public prints,[12] and, on the whole, approve of the way their university deals with value-problems and value inculcation.[13] It is not our impression that these evaluations are naively uncritical resultants of blissful ignorance; rather, the generality of these students find their university experience congenial to their own sense of values.

Students are approximately equally divided between those who regard vocational preparation as the primary goal of an ideal education and those who chose a general liberal education.

---

[12] An exception: a large proportion admit the justice of charges of "production-line teaching." And who would gainsay them on this point?

[13] Criticisms are made by the students mainly of value-areas which they themselves rank as low in importance in the educational goals of a university, e.g., marriage and family life, community problems, development of moral values and personal character.

Other conceivable goals, such as character-education and social adjustment, are of secondary importance to them. *The ideal of a liberal education impresses itself upon the students more and more as they move through college.* Even in such technical curricula as engineering, the senior is much more likely than the freshman to choose, as an ideal, liberal education over specific vocational preparation. In the university milieu of scholarship and research, of social diversity, of new ideas and varied and wide-ranging interests, "socialization" into a campus culture apparently means heightened appreciation of the idea of a liberal education in the arts and sciences.

Students' *choices* of ideal educational goals *are not arbitrary or whimsical.* There is a clear relationship between their educational evaluations and their basic pattern of general values. The selective and directional qualities of basic value-orientations are clearly evident in these data: the "success-oriented" students choose vocational preparation, the "other-directed" choose goals of social adjustment ("getting along with people"), the "intellectuals" choose a liberal arts emphasis.

The same patterned consistency shows itself in occupational choices.[14] There is *impressive consistency between specific occupational preferences and the student's basic conception of what is for him a good way of life.* And, contrary to many popular assertions, the *goal-values chosen do not seem to us to be primarily oriented to materialistic success nor to mere conformity.* Our students want occupations that permit them to use their talents and training, to be creative and original, to work with and to help other people. They also want money, prestige, and security. But they are *optimistic about their prospects* in these regards; they set *limits to their aspirations* — few aspire to millions of dollars or to "imperial" power and glory. Within the fixed frame of these aspirations, they can afford to place a high

[14] Morris Rosenberg (1958).

value on the expressive and people-oriented aspects of occupation and to minimize the instrumental-reward values of power, prestige, and wealth.

Occupational choices are also useful — and interesting — in bringing out clearly that values do not constitute the only component in goals and aspirations. For there is also the "face of reality" in the form of the individual's perceptions of his own abilities and interests, of the objective possibilities open to him, of the familial and other social pressures to which he is exposed. We find "reluctant recruits" whose values are not in line with their expected occupation's characteristics. Students develop occupational images — not always accurate or detailed — and they try to fit their values to the presumed characteristics of the imagined occupation. The purely cognitive or informational problems are often acute. Furthermore, many reluctant recruits are yielding to social demands, or compromising in the face of their own limitations of opportunity, or of ability and performance. Thus, many a creativity-oriented aspirant for a career in architecture, drama, or journalism, resigns himself to a real estate business; many a people-oriented student who dreams of the M.D. decides to enter his father's advertising agency; and many a hopeful incipient business executive decides it were better to teach the theory of business administration than to practice it. The old ideal of the independent entrepreneur is extant — but so is the recognition that the main chance may be in a corporate bureaucracy.

In their views on dating, courtship, sex, and family life, our students prefer what they are expected to prefer. For them, in the grim words of a once-popular song, love and marriage go together like a horse and carriage. Their expressed standards concerning sex roles, desirable age for marriage, characteristics of an ideal mate, number of children desired are congruent with the values and stereotypes of the preceding generation — minus compulsive rebellion. They even accept the "double standard" of sex morality in a double sense, i.e., both sexes agree that standards for men differ from standards for women, and women apply to both sexes a standard different from that held by men.

"Conservatism" and "traditionalism" seem implied by what has just been said. But these terms are treacherous. *In the field of political values, it is certainly true that students are not radical, not rebels against their parents or their peers.*[15] And as they go through college, the students tend to bring their political position in line with that prevalent in the social groups to which they belong. Yet they have accepted most of the extant "welfare state" provisions for health, security, and the regulation of economic affairs, and they overwhelmingly approve of the traditional "liberalism" of the Bill of Rights. When their faith in civil liberties is tested against strong pressures of social expediency in specific issues, e.g., suppression of "dangerous ideas," many waver and give in. The students who are most willing to acquiesce in the suppression of civil liberties are also those who are most likely to be prejudiced against minority groups, to be conformist and traditionalistic in general social attitudes, and to lack a basic faith in people.

As one looks at the existing evidence, one finds a correlation, although only a slight one, between high grades and "libertarian" values. But the correlation is substantial only among upperclassmen. In other words, as students go through college, those who are most successful academically tend to become more committed to a "Bill of Rights" orientation. College in gross — just the general experience — may have varying effects, but *the students who are successful emerge with strengthened and clarified democratic values.* This finding is consistent also with the fact that student leaders are more likely to be supporters of the values implicit in civil liberties than the other students.

There is now substantial evidence from several major studies

[15] "The college student body of today overwhelmingly shies away from political extremism." American Council on Education (1958), p. 116.

of college students that *the experience of the college years results in a certain, selective homogenization of attitudes and values.* Detached from their prior statuses and social groups and exposed to the pervasive stimuli of the university milieu, the students tend to assimilate a new common *culture,* to converge toward norms characteristic of their own particular campus. Furthermore, in certain respects, there are norms common to colleges and universities across the country. For instance, college-educated people consistently show up in study after study as more often than others supporters of the Bill of Rights and other democratic rights and liberties. The interesting thing in this connection is that the norms upon which students tend to converge include toleration of diversity.

To the extent that our sampling of the orientations of American college students in the years 1950 and 1952 may be representative of our culture — and still valid in 1959 — *we are disposed to question the summary characterization of the current generation as silent, beat, apathetic,* or as a mass of other-directed conformists who are guided solely by social radar without benefit of inner gyroscopes. Our data indicate that these students of today do basically accept the existing institutions of the society, and, in the face of the realities of complex and large-scale economic and political problems, make a wary and ambivalent delegation of trust to those who occupy positions of legitimized responsibility for coping with such collective concerns. *In a real sense they are admittedly conservative,* but their conservatism incorporates a traditionalized embodiment of the original "radicalism" of 1776. Although we have no measures of its strength or intensity, the heritage of the doctrine of inalienable rights is retained. As they move through the college years our young men and women are "socialized" into a broadly similar culture, at the level of personal behavior. In this sense also, they are surely conformists. It is even true that some among them use the sheer fact of conformity — "everyone does it" — as a criterion for conduct. But the extent of ethical robotism is easily overestimated. Few students are really so faceless in the not-so-lonely crowd of the swelling population in our institutions of higher learning. And it may be well to recall that to say "conformity" is, in part, another way of saying "orderly human society."

In the field of religious beliefs and values, the college students seem to faithfully reflect the surrounding culture. Their commitments are, for the most part, couched in a familiar idiom. *Students testify to a felt need for a religious faith or ultimate personal philosophy. Avowed atheists or freethinkers are so rare as to be a curiosity.* The religious quest is often intense and deep, and there are students on every campus who are seriously wrestling with the most profound questions of meaning and value. At the same time, a major proportion of these young men and women see religion as a means of personal adjustment, an anchor for family life, a source of emotional security. These personal and social goals often overshadow the goals of intellectual clarity, and spiritual transcendence. The "cult of adjustment" does exist. It exists alongside the acceptance of traditional forms of organized religion (church, ordained personnel, ritual, dogma). Still another segment of the student population consists of those who seek, in what they regard as religion, intellectual clarity, rational belief, and ethical guidance and reinforcement.

Our first impression of the data was that the students were surprisingly orthodox and religiously involved. Upon second thought we were forced to realize that we have very few reliable historical benchmarks against which we might compare the present situation, and that conclusions that present-day students are "more" or "less" religious could not be defended on the basis of our data.[16] As we looked more intently at the con-

[16] Other research suggests that "orthodox" belief has increased among college students. See A. R. Gilliland (1953), pp. 113-16.

tent of belief and the extent of religious participation, we received the impression that many of the religious convictions expressed represented a conventional acceptance, of low intensity. But, here again, comparative benchmarks are lacking, and we do not know, in any case, what measure of profoundity and intensity to expect from healthy, young, secure and relatively inexperienced persons; after all, feelings of immortality and invulnerability are standard illusions of youth. Nor are optimistic and socially-oriented themes at all rare in the distinctive religious history of this country.

Kluckhohn recently has summarized evidence regarding changes in values during a period of years, primarily 1935-1955, but extending much farther back in some instances.[17] A variety of data are assembled to bear upon such alleged changes as diminished puritan morality, work-success ethic, individualism, achievement, lessened emphasis on future-time orientation in favor of sociability, moral relativism, consideration and tolerance, conformity, hedonistic present-time orientation. Although he questions the extent and nature of the alleged revival of religion and the alleged increase in conformity, and thinks that "hedonistic" present-time orientation does not have the meaning usually attributed to it, he does conclude that Americans increasingly enjoy leisure without guilt, do not stress achievement so much as formerly, are more accepting of group harmony as a goal, more tolerant of diversity and aware of other cultures. He sees an active search for explicit values.

The findings just presented do not imply that there are no important differences of opinion among students; on the contrary, there are sharp and deep-going divisions on both public issues and personal style of life. These differences are found in each of the student bodies studied, and there are marked group differences among the various universities: Harvard is not the same as the University of Texas; Wayne is not Wesleyan.

[17] Clyde Kluckhohn, in Elting E. Morrison (1958), pp. 158-204.

If these data are to be trusted at all, contemporary college students are not anything like the uniform mass of contented and unquestioning conformists they are sometimes represented to be. Differences in *values* — not just particular topical opinions — are expressed in occupational choices, educational goals, religious convictions, political opinions, choice of living unit at college, and views of family life and sex roles.

On the other hand, it is equally true that these differences tend to remain within relatively fixed margins, and that marked alienation from, or rebellion against, existing institutions and the values implicated in them is exceedingly rare. The most marked effect associated with the college years is a crystallization, polarization, and factual and conceptual elaboration of the widely-shared values with which the student enters upon higher education.

For the great majority of these young people, their society, so far, has been "good to them." Despite cold war and vast threats, their social environment has been in many ways more nurturant and permissive than that experienced by the "depression generation"; in a certain real sense they have less against which to rebel. It is possible that their orientation may result in less than maximal intellectual tension and vigorous and disciplined educational activity. But it would be easy to leap to unjustified conclusions, and we prefer for the moment the Scotch verdict of "not proven."

In closing, perhaps one may be permitted to take leave of the research data to record the impression, perhaps speculative, that the values the students bring to education are not only "American" but also "Western" and also to some extent "universal." In their strivings for clarity, structure, self-knowledge, humane understandings, and sense of the scope and meaning of life, they often give us glimpses of great potentialities. We certainly may be allowed to hope that our educational system will increasingly help them to live under larger skies.

John J. Kane is Professor of Sociology at the University of Notre Dame and head of the department since 1951; president of the American Catholic Sociological Society, 1952; *member of many professional societies and also active in associations such as* NAACP, National Conference of Christians and Jews; *author of* Marriage and the Family: A Catholic Approach, *1952;* Protestant-Catholic Conflicts in America, *1955; many publications in the areas of minorities (racial and religious), juvenile delinquency and education.*

John J. Kane

QUESTIONS OF VALUE

CHOICE IN EDUCATION

THE BROAD PERSPECTIVE OF VALUES IN EDUCATION, SUCH AS that made so effectively by Professor Williams, makes criticism of the total range hardly feasible here. But some of what we may hopefully consider to be the more salient points will be reviewed and evaluated here.

While admitting that social change has occurred, Professor Williams seems to indicate that in the realm of values at least, such change has been more a matter of degree than of kind. The American of the present bears a definite family resemblance to the American of the past, and probably of the future. Yet, he has remarked that the inevitable "relevance of values" in all inquiry, scientific or otherwise, was certainly not an acceptable notion just a short generation ago.

Here is a notable change both in values and about values, and its implications for the field of education are tremendous. No doubt the issue here is upon what values or value-systems education shall be based. Obviously in a pluralistic society there will be, as there are today, various kinds of values and consequently various kinds of education. Unless the cult of conformity becomes widespread, which Professor Williams seems to intimate is not occurring to the extent we have been led to believe, diversity in educational philosophies will persist. Perhaps this is inevitable in a society characterized by mass education. Furthermore, while in the not so recent past the relevance of values to inquiry was indeed denied on the verbal level, it was practiced on the actual level — by the very persons who denied it. In fact, refusal to grant the relevance of values was a value in itself.

VALUE RELEVANCE AND CONFLICT

An intriguing aspect of the remarks by Professor Williams about the relevance of values to science, education and particularly social science merits comment. To what extent shall science, education and social science establish values? If they do establish them at all, what kinds of values will these be? One may distinguish between proximate and ultimate values. For example, educators may decide that it is wise for students to have a speaking knowledge of foreign languages. This is a criterion or standard which may be considered desirable in view of America's position of world leadership, the necessity of knowing and understanding other peoples.

But ultimate values, the standards by which men live, the rightness or wrongness of an act, man's final destiny, are values from the fields of philosophy and theology. Education and science cannot neglect them, but neither can they establish them. Certainly in the past this proposition has not been acceptable.

While the point is made that the dominant value-themes of American society were selective and incomplete, they do represent clear, concise and accurate portrayals of some of the very important American values. The intensity with which they are held throughout the society, and specific variations within ethnic or religious groups are open to some debate. Yet their influence on American education is clear. In fact, it is so clear that one readily recognizes, even in schools maintained by religious denominations with heavy commitments to speculative thought, that the vocational aspect of education frequently at least challenges if it does not quite outstrip the humanities.

Under the conflict of values the question is raised about the amount of custodial effort manifest in our colleges and universities. This is certain to stimulate discussion. Custodial may sound like a harsh word, albeit such was not intended, but it does seem apt. To be even franker about it, if colleges and universities are furthering the maturation of students emotionally, are they not also victims of value-conflicts themselves? Excessive custodial care may mean that faculties and administrations have somewhat less faith than they proclaim in the education process. Perhaps this is a type of "alma momism" to which psychiatrists may turn their attention. It is understood by some commencement speakers who inform a college graduating class that it is now about to enter the world. Unfortunately, at times these speakers may be only too correct.

The dilemma between teaching and research is, as has often been stated, one of emphasis. It is also persistent and not readily solved. Here one encounters what may be termed a hierarchy of values, varying from one institution to another. Ideally, most college professors should be involved in teaching and research, but if the latter is disproportionately rewarded and the former is relatively disregarded, those who can will do research; those who can't will teach. In the most extreme of such cases the professor will be better known to scholarly colleagues in his field than to the students in his classroom.

Current controversy over the so-called life adjustment courses is possibly a synthetic value-conflict. Without doubt there are extremes to which such courses can go and extremists who would push them there. In the broadest and best sense of the term, life adjustment, almost any course of respectable content at the college level would or should contribute something to the life adjustment of the student. Certainly philosophy, religion, psychology and many areas of social science either directly or indirectly may do so. Furthermore, a great deal of values for adjustment may be caught by the student rather than taught, depending on the character, personality and dedication of the respective professor.

Professor Williams' comment — "there are modes of education for personal adjustment and group adaptation that seem to involve severe sacrifices in individuality" — should also merit serious attention. The hidden persuaders do not employ devices whose limitations are strictly confined to the sale of popcorn and coke in motion picture theaters. Far less attention has been given this matter than it deserves. Certain techniques in social psychology, for example, seem to come dangerously close to manipulation of individuals. While the goals of some of the experiments reported are innocuous and even at times desirable, they need not always be. Fortunately, their success is somewhat less than sometimes claimed for them.

Value-conflicts over the extent to which education should be secular or religious are compelling ones. It is a problem that has perplexed and will continue to perplex those involved in education, not to mention the courts. The American heritage includes religion. Insofar as education is the transmission of this heritage, shall religion be excluded? But again in a land of religious pluralism, just what shall be taught? As Professor Williams indicated, to date the complex distinction between what is religious and what is secular has not been satisfactorily made. One public high school principal was criticized for permitting the organist to play *Onward Christian Soldiers* at the commencement exercise. Yet, in some places baccalaureate services are held for public school children in churches. In one case when students of a certain religious persuasion failed to attend, they were not awarded their diplomas at the commencement held later in the high school.

A COMPARISON OF VALUES

It is possible to make some limited comparison between

the data gathered in the Cornell study and a 5 per cent sample of Notre Dame students in the Arts and Letters College who responded to part of the Cornell questionnaire. Like students in the Cornell study Notre Dame men overwhelmingly approve of the job their university is doing academically; and perhaps even more interesting is the almost three to one response agreeing with most of the rules and regulations in force at Notre Dame. While no material is available for students in the Colleges of Engineering, Science, and Commerce, over half of the Arts and Letters sample was success-oriented, although these students had not chosen vocational preparation.

Just as students in the study reported by Professor Williams had resigned themselves to the real estate business or abandoned medicine for advertising, almost one out of every four students in the Notre Dame study had changed majors. In most cases these changes would not have been so far-reaching, since only a few students had moved from another college to Arts and Letters. Yet there probably are one or two who formerly aspired to medicine or engineering.

Evidence from the study here likewise seems to question current claims that today's college youth are silent, beat or apathetic. On the contrary, they seem to have considerable assurance. Most of the time most of them are in good spirits or fairly good spirits, rather rarely are upset, and only 10 per cent think they are doing poorly in their college work. They rather modestly admit by a ratio of almost seven to one that they have lived up to what their parents expected either very well or fairly well.

Some of their beliefs are also quite traditional. They consider ability on the job and conscientious, hard work the best way to succeed in the armed forces. On the other hand they say that hard work and, next to this, a pleasant personality are the ways for a young person to get ahead most quickly today. They are certainly not conformists. When in a group most of them prefer to make decisions themselves. Less than 1 per cent usually prefers to have others make decisions for them.

Yet they do show one sign of relative apathy in that most of them do not get worked up about what happens in politics or public affairs as they would about what happens in their personal lives.

It is not possible to draw any broad-scale conclusions from the data and evidence of this study, but the results do suggest considerable similarity in values between students in a Catholic institution and those at other institutions. With such a background it may be proposed that what Professor Williams has so provocatively presented may be a far more accurate picture of college-student values than some of the pessimists in our midst now give. For this reversal of interpretative principles, rooted as it is in empirical research, we can be singularly grateful.

4

Values and
American Economic Life

Joseph P. Fitzpatrick, S.J., is Associate Professor of Sociology, Fordham University; past president of the American Catholic Sociological Society, 1953; major writing and research areas in industrial, rural and urban sociology and comparative institutions; some recent publications have focused on labor relations and minorities, such as Puerto Ricans in the United States.

Joseph P. Fitzpatrick, S.J.

INDIVIDUALISM IN
AMERICAN INDUSTRY

PROBABLY THE MOST STRIKING THING ABOUT THE VALUES OF American economic life today is the extent to which they are being subjected to study and analysis. Just a few years ago the National Council of Churches completed a careful study of the "Ethics and Economics of Society," a painstaking effort to uncover the ethical values at work in American business life.[1] At the present time, the Harvard Business School continues its inquiries into the ethics of business life during the Danforth summer seminars. And every year sees the publication of a number of volumes devoted to the same kind of discussion and analysis as the one in which we are engaged here.[2]

It is not altogether clear whether this is a sign of health or weakness. Christopher Dawson once made the remark: "Happy the nation without a history; and thrice happy the nation without a sociology, because, when a nation has become conscious

---

[1] The publications which issued from this study are well known: A. Dudley Ward (1952), Kenneth E. Boulding (1953), Howard R. Bowen (1953), Ward, Leavy and Freedman (1953), Bowen, *et al.* (1954). See also Childs and Cater (1954).

[2] Some of the more important ones in recent years: Whyte (1956), Bell (1956), Drucker (1957), Sutton, *et al.* (1956), Lerner (1957), Selekman and Selekman (1956). Perhaps the most controversial has been Galbraith (1958).

of itself, it has begun to decay." Dawson was suggesting that our social life was something like our stomach. While it is functioning properly, we are unaware of it. Only when things go wrong is our attention called painfully to its existence. On the other hand, we are aware that reflection and analysis bring into our consciousness the subtle influences on our behavior and enable us to take a more intelligent responsibility over our actions. Our concern over values, therefore, may represent the decay of our society painfully impressing itself on our consciousness; or it may represent our own maturity in penetrating to the hidden motivations in our economic life so that we may better control them and guide them consciously to chosen goals. I am still optimistic enough to believe that the second interpretation is the correct one.

The most fruitful direction for our study, it seems to me, should be toward the dilemma which has been featured in many recent analyses of our economic life.[3] It may be stated thus: Certain fundamental values, such as individualism and freedom, were the driving force behind the economic developments of the United States. But the vigorous pursuit of those values has gradually led to the creation of a system which makes the perpetuation of those values difficult if not impossible. The pursuit of freedom in free enterprise has created a highly complicated system of organizations in which freedom is severely limited; the pursuit of individualism has led to forms of association in which the individual is almost completely dependent on the group. From Elton Mayo's worker[4] who suffers from being too much by himself and whose satisfying social relationships have been shattered by the machine, to William H. Whyte's organization man whose satisfaction comes from fitting himself in as a faithful cog in the management machine, descriptions of American industrial life are not marked by the opti-

[3] A good summary of the discussion can be found in Katzell (1958).
[4] Elton Mayo (1945).

mistic assertion that it provides opportunity for personal freedom and individual development.

In the presence of this dilemma, I should like to propose a few questions for consideration.

1) Is this really a case in which ideas and values have created a social and economic organization which in turn is destroying them? Or have the ideas and values changed regardless of the social and economic organization? Or were the ideas and values simply rationalizations, the unreality of which is being revealed to us in the consequences of less noble values which were never frankly acknowledged?

2) If the values which provided the drive that developed American industry can no longer find expression, does this imply that we are reaching the end of our great achievement?

Or is it truer to say that, under the impact of events, and in response to extraordinary social and cultural changes, the traditional values are expressing themselves in a new way within the framework of a social and economic structure in which the old definitions no longer have any meaning? It is clear what individualism meant to a pioneer farmer in Oklahoma a century ago. But what does individualism mean to a clerk in the Chase-Manhattan Bank or to a member of the Board of Directors of General Motors?

3) If the great motivation for our past achievement came from the values of individualism and freedom, and if it is true that these values cannot find expression today, what values will supply the motivation and the drive for the tasks of the future?

VALUES AND INDIVIDUALISM

By values, I mean those ideals, goals, norms which guide man's behavior; according to which he judges whether his behavior is right or wrong; which lead toward the betterment of himself and his fellow men, or toward their detriment; which enable him to discriminate between that which is good and that which is bad.[5] I take it for granted that, traditionally, the central value in our economic life was individualism: the idea that everything must be done to give each individual the freedom to achieve the fulfillment of which he is capable. Competition, freedom, success, equal opportunity, I consider subordinate to this major value. The early image of our society was of a kind of free atmosphere in which each individual was to find his own level by his own effort. This individualism was intimately related to personal responsibility. It was directed toward the rational mastery of man's environment in which the discipline of work played a major moral role, and in which material rewards became a sign not only of business ability but of moral virtue.

This individualism resulted in the conviction that the welfare and interests of the community, the "common good," would be served best when each individual pursued his own development. In other words, the good community was precisely the community that enabled each individual to perfect himself. This statement of values was quite contrary to traditional moral teaching in the West before the rise of what is commonly termed the "Protestant ethic." Traditional moral teaching insisted that economic activity must serve the common welfare; that the individual perfected himself by the pursuit of justice, that is, by practicing a form of economic behavior which served the needs of the community rather than his own interest. Whereas in one, the common welfare was consequent upon an individual's effort to perfect himself; in the other the individual's perfection was consequent upon his effort to serve the needs of the community. The earlier moral tradition,[6] therefore, insisted that the economy be given direction by moral and spir-

[5] For a very good presentation of the nature of values, see Williams (1951), chap. II.

[6] For a good review of the principles of this earlier moral tradition and its contemporary restatement, see Cronin (1950).

itual norms. According to Tawney[7] and Fanfani,[8] it was precisely the weakening of these moral and spiritual norms that
enabled a free economy to develop which blossomed in industrial capitalism, and in the social evils which resulted from
the pursuit of individual gain. In the restatement of these
moral principles contemporary religious leaders still insist that
social evils will continue to beset modern economic life until
it is given direction by clear moral norms.

This moral issue is not the issue which the present paper
discusses directly. It was the issue in the studies of economic
life by the National Council of Churches. It has been the issue
in the many statements of Catholic spokesmen about our modern
business system. And this issue was given rather vigorous expression in the statement in *Fortune*[9] in 1958 by Rabbi Louis
Finkelstein that individualism cannot be the moral value directing economic activity. American businessmen, nonetheless, still
strongly assert the value of individualism. While American businessmen may assert this, they have shown nevertheless, a remarkably realistic ability to adjust their activities to a number
of growing pressures which have compelled them to relate their
economic activities increasingly to the common welfare.

The issue which the present paper will discuss is the change
in the total situation of business activity in the United States,
and the reaction which this change has had on the traditional
values of our culture.

STRUCTURAL AND SITUATIONAL CHANGES

There are any number of ways of analyzing the structural
and situational changes of American industry and economic life.
Organization and the effects of organization are the usual foci
around which the analysis proceeds. I have singled out a few

[7] Tawney (1926).
[8] Fanfani (1946).
[9] Finkelstein (1958).

of these changes which have been the occasion of new insights into the nature of American industry, or which have provoked a new judgment upon it. The ones I have singled out are not necessarily the most important, but they will provide a convenient setting for our later discussion.

1) First there is the culmination of our technological development in the achievement of a white-collar society. In 1956, for the first time the number of white-collar workers exceeded the number of blue-collar workers in the United States. This would seem to indicate that the United States has at last achieved what has often been represented as the American Dream. But it is precisely the technology of this white-collar world which seems most to threaten us with a loss of individualism, with excessive conformity, with over-organization. It is in relation to this white-collar world that much of the most serious criticism of contemporary values has been raised.[10]

2) Subordinate to this has been the increasing emphasis, aided and abetted by sociologists and applied anthropologists, on "human relations in industry." This again has been a highly controversial development. It is represented by some as a refined and polite expression of old and not very honorable values of American business. It has been extolled by others as the expression of new values, an appreciation of the role of the human person in industrial life.[11]

3) On the much larger scale of the relationship of industry to society, an important situational change is the role that American industry has come to play in national defense. The advertising of American industry has boasted very forcefully about this as a proof of the altruism of American business. The altruism has a high content of personal interest, but actually

[10] Mills (1951) has a bitter criticism of the new middle class; also see Riesman (1950). For an analysis of the changes in the economic system see Drucker (1949) and (1957).

[11] For a summary of the controversy, see Moore (1951), pp. 197-200.

we have come to realize vividly that the primary importance of American industrial activity is not to provide us with conveniences, but to provide us with security against an enemy that is remarkably equipped technically. It would be foolish to attribute this entirely to American industry since it is the result of a convergence of many of our resources from the efforts of the scientist in the university laboratory, to the planning of the expert civil servant, to the production of workingmen on the assembly lines. The important shift is the fact that the image of industry is no longer only that of an enterprise which aggressive men are directing for their own self-interest; it is also the image of a skillful productive achievement where the efforts of many devoted public servants converge to produce the equipment and missiles necessary for our survival and the survival of the free world. Although this is the world directed by what C. Wright Mills criticizes as "The Power Elite," nevertheless, in the public mind, it is not pictured as a selfish adventure, but as part of a giant complex which represents an extraordinary national effort for our defense.

4) A fourth situational change is the relationship of industry to rapid population growth in many areas of the world, and the realization that industry is one of the essential elements involved in the effort to enable the population to survive. Industrial organization in this context does not signify individual enterprise for profit. Rather it signifies a reorganization of physical and human resources which will enable a large number of people to live comfortably where smaller numbers, without industry, found it difficult even to survive. Although this concept of industry pertains mainly to underdeveloped areas, it has served also to give us a new and deeper insight into the relationship of industry to our own society.

5) A fifth situational change has been the phenomenal development of industry in the Soviet Union. This has led to a realization that a highly efficient industrial and technological

structure can be developed without any democratic values involved. In other words, as Drucker points out so clearly in *The New Society,* the structure is quite distinct from the values to which it may be related in a particular society. Therefore, the significant thing about American industry is not the fact that it has been developed. It could have been developed, apparently, in nations with much different ideologies than our own. The significant thing must be the values for which the men created it. This places a stress on values where it was not exactly placed before.

If each of these situational changes is examined carefully, it indicates a change in American industry — either a change in which the old values of American life cannot readily be expressed; or in which they are being expressed in a new way.

THE WHITE-COLLAR SOCIETY

The coming of the white-collar world reflects the great increase in automation, in technical skills, in methods of production that enable men to control production rather than be immersed in it. But it is precisely this white-collar world that is the world of huge and complicated organization. This world is bitterly criticized by C. Wright Mills for fostering hypocrisy and alienation; for engendering a host of social parasites whose status is borrowed instead of being earned by the assertion of their own value and merit. It is the world of "other-directed men"; of the over-organization that Nisbet speaks about that makes "community" impossible;[12] it is the world of Eric Fromm's dependent, impoverished, uncreative man.[13]

Unless we had witnessed it, it would have been impossible to imagine such a flood of criticism loosed upon the achieve-

[12] Nisbet (1953).
[13] Fromm (1955).

ment of our great American economic virtues. Without over-looking in the least some of the serious problems connected with American industry, nevertheless there are many ways in which our present condition can be interpreted not only as the fulfillment of American virtues, but as a new framework within which they will be given even more fruitful expression. It did not require a John Galbraith to assure us that modern American industry has gone far toward conquering poverty by solving the problem of production. Complicated organization has placed in man's hands the possibility of extraordinary achievements; and the new technology offers man for the first time the opportunity of controlling the machine rather than being controlled by it. But man's fulfillment in such a system will be consequent on his development on a wide scale of what I call the "organization virtues."

Let me take first the problem of the alienation of work. The meaning of work and the satisfactions of labor have generally been associated with the work of the individual. These satisfactions, if they are to be realized, must now be realized through a group. It is very possible that writers in the past have romanticized the satisfaction and meaning of work. Craftsmen were always a small minority. Hard toil was the ordinary lot of ordinary men. What gave men satisfaction was not a particular form of work; but a relationship between their work and society, the cultural value attributed to what they were doing that gave them a sense of achievement. The almost brutal struggle of Irish fishermen against the Western sea would have been a kind of crude drudgery were it not for the great value of achievement, of mastery which the culture of the Irish coast associated with it. The wearisome toil of the sugar-cane worker under the tropical sun could easily have been defined as inhuman, but the culture associated this with masculine prowess, and the responsibility of a man for the support of his family.

There have been cultures in which what we consider the noble work of the craftsman was considered an inferior kind of human occupation. It was not so much the particular nature of the work itself, as the cultural setting in which the work had a definite meaning that led to the satisfaction and sense of accomplishment of the working man. Therefore there seems to be no reason why organized forms of work could not become related to values in our society that would give them great meaning. Certainly anyone who has anything remotely to do with the construction of a Jupiter rocket or a jet plane must have had some sense of achievement in seeing even a picture of the outcome of his work. It does not seem to be too much to expect that the higher education demanded by a white-collar society would enable people to be more reflective about their part in organized activity, and derive a great satisfaction out of the ultimate results of the over-all groups of which they are small parts.

Another aspect of "group virtues" stems from the fact that so much of man's welfare, intellectual as well as material, now rests upon the effective functioning of organization. Therefore, important spiritual and psychological developments will have to become related to the development of those values and virtues which will enable men to participate effectively in organization. If a "Protestant ethic" sparked the outburst of individual effort and individual responsibility in the early days of capitalism when man's social welfare depended on individual effort, could it not be expected to spark a similar responsibility for group effort when social welfare has come to depend on collective effort. This is the area in which man conforms, as Riesman puts it, intelligently and freely rather than compulsively. It seemed to me that Whyte, in his overemphasis on a kind of conformity which is related to selfish interests and personal convenience, may have overlooked the highly responsible conformity which enables an organization to achieve remarkable objectives. The administration of government, the production of food to feed the rapidly growing population of the world, national defense, protection of health, the exploration of space — these and many other things so pressing in modern life, can come only from conformity, the conformity of men with that kind of behavior which is necessary to enable huge organizations to function well. To say that modern organization is "inhuman" because it has done violence to what are called the "natural" relationships of men, is a very understandable reaction, but not a very helpful one. It seems more important to recognize that personal responsibility and personal fulfillment can be achieved by man's reflective and intelligent participation in the highly complicated group activity of the present day.

HUMAN RELATIONS IN INDUSTRY

Intimately related to this question of organizational behavior is the question of the role of the human person in the industrial situation. The effort of industrial sociologists, anthropologists, psychologists to analyze and explain the behavior of men in bureaucratic structures has been one of the significant developments of modern social science. It has been called, in some quarters, "managerial sociology," a method of manipulating working people to do the will of the employer enthusiastically and efficiently in situations in which, without good human relations, they might resist very strongly. Whereas poverty compelled the co-operation of poor immigrants a century ago, perhaps skill in human relations can manipulate the co-operation of more sophisticated Americans today. In either case, business is pictured as a system in which a large number of subordinates are working under a form of either very open or very subtle compulsion to achieve the objectives of business leaders. Indeed there is a certain legitimacy in picturing American business as a system that flourished in the past by taking advantage of the economic need of poor people. In this sense, if one wishes to follow this unfavorable interpretation of business history, and the equally unfavorable interpretation of industrial sociology, he could say that "managerial sociology" represents a continuation of traditional values of American management.

But I really think that the interest in human relations represents something much more positive than this. It represents, in many aspects, a recognition that the human factor, just like so many other factors of the environment, must be dealt with rationally; and dealing with a man rationally implies the acknowledgment of the man's personal needs, values and satisfactions. This leads to a willingness to accept methods of acquiring the co-operation of the person by enabling him to achieve his personal needs and satisfactions, and to pursue his personal values as much as is possible within the framework of a complicated organization. It is precisely this ability to adjust to the inevitable, to come to terms with the obvious demands of the situation that has always represented a great value in American industrial life.

I have no doubt that "good human relations" on the part of many a manager are highly colored with self-interest, with the desire to increase profits, with the hope of avoiding the inconvenience of a union. But self-interest has always played a vital part in American business life. The significance of the value of self-interest in America is precisely the fact that it has adjusted itself so effectively to new situations and to new insights into situations.

I do not think that any better example of this adjustment can be found than the gradual recognition of the labor union in American industry and the development of employer-employee relations. The labor movement, with all its violence and conflict, has been the institution that has compelled American industry to come to terms with the human values of employees. I certainly think that theory of the labor union is correct which explains it as a thoroughly American institution, the banding together of free men in order to gain for themselves their rightful status as first-class citizens of our industrial society. With all its strong opposition to the labor unions and the antagonism that is still deep in the minds of many businessmen, American industry has come to accept the principle of unionism as genuinely American. This adjustment is an excellent example of the ability of American businessmen to accept not only the inevitable, but to adjust themselves to what they come to see as a rightful part of American life.[14]

INDUSTRY AND NATIONAL DEFENSE

It is impossible for anyone to think of American industry today the way he thought of it before World War II. Industry has always played an important role in war; some industries have profited wonderfully from it. But the nature of international conflict today and the crucial role that American industry has come to play in defense has served to bring into sharp focus the social and cultural context in which industry operates today. The interrelationship of science, government and industry outlines the role of industry much more sharply as having the characteristics of a national institution rather than those of a private enterprise. And today, soldier, citizen, government official and business leader realize the quasi-public nature of these giant organizations, and the responsibility that government and the public must exercise with reference to them if the public welfare is to be served.

This is a context in which individualism and freedom must be defined anew. Just as the study of science has taken on the aura of a national responsibility within the past few years,

[14] Much more discussion should be given to the extraordinary role of the labor union in American life. Present limitations of space forbid this, but one can consult: *Fortune* (1951), Slichter (1948), Bakke (1947). For a summary review of theories, see Perlman (1958).

likewise the pursuit of business must relate the fulfillment of the individual to the service of the community, and channel his freedom into directions much more clearly defined by the demands of the nation at large. Thirty years ago, when a young man decided to study physics, he did so because he liked it, or was interested in it, or thought he could make some money out of it. He still probably thinks the same things. But these values now operate within a context in which he can never be unmindful of the relationship of his own mastery of science to the destiny of the free world. It is in this same sense that I refer to the new attitude toward business. The same motives of achievement, power and wealth are still a major factor in American business, but the businessmen with these motivations can never be unmindful of national security which creates a different dimension for the fulfillment of his individual effort and marks out more sharply the boundaries of his freedom.

I have in mind here the wonderful insight that anthropologists and sociologists have been giving us into the nature of economic pursuits, namely, that industrial activity is not the completely free behavior of men who freely and consciously choose this for reasons that are clear to them; rather, industrial activity is the expression of a culture and always involves motivations and values of which we are not always aware. What I have suggested above is that this insight is being impressed upon the minds of Americans today by the role of industry in defense. Life is so intimately intertwined and our interdependence is so clear, that industrial activity reveals itself more clearly as the cultural behavior of a whole people; as the expression of a state of mind that is shared by those outside of industry as well as in; as a form of activity which is much more in the nature of a national effort than the achievement of a rugged individual.

In this context, therefore, individualism and freedom are given new definitions and express themselves in quite a new way.

If they can express themselves successfully they will lead to achievements much more noble than that of the titans who looked so proudly on the early industrial giants as worlds of their own creation.

INDUSTRY AND UNDERDEVELOPED AREAS

It is mainly in relation to the previous point that one sees the importance of the issue of industry and its relationship to areas of rapid population growth. This is another development which has given us a new insight into the nature of industry as part of man's response to his environment. In other words, industry is not simply a technical activity which some men can engage in for their own achievement or profit. Industry is something that we begin to see as essential in relating men to each other and in relating men to material resources. There simply has to be industrial development if growing populations are going to survive. The development of industry, therefore, is not conceived as an area where an individual competes for advancement or fulfillment; it is conceived as part of the social process of a developing or developed society, something that has to be there whether individuals provide it or the State. Achievement in this context is seen not in terms of the prowess an individual can demonstrate, nor in terms of what an individual can make of it, but in terms of its vital relationship to a population as one of the important factors that keep them alive.

Again, in relation to the industrializing of underdeveloped areas, the social sciences have given us remarkable insights into the social processes which are involved, into the distressing effects this can have in the disorganization of cultures. But the effort is always toward an intelligent introduction of industry that will gradually become integrated into the culture; not an effort to prevent it.

This growing awareness of the importance of industry in

other parts of the world has clarified our idea of industry as an institution of the community, intimately related to the community's life, and not an arena where individuals could be free to compete for advancement or gain. Together with our own experience with American industry and its relation to security, this realization of the importance of industry as an essential part of a growing society's life have helped us to recognize that individualism and freedom, now confined to group action, can make a contribution to the welfare of a society far more important than the personal achievement of an isolated individual competing for business success.

THE INDUSTRIALIZATION OF THE SOVIET UNION

Finally, and briefly, the extraordinary industrial achievements of Russia have caused us to make a sharp distinction between industry itself and the values which are at work in relation to it. For a long time, there had been the impression that American individualism and American freedom were the values that had been responsible for industrial development; that, unless men had been free to compete for their self-interest, the great complex of technology and industry would never have arisen. In fact, according to Sutton's work, *The American Business Creed,* there are still a great many businessmen who believe this. This led to a very close identification of American values with particular forms of industrial organization and achievement. American industry was the creation of free men.

However, when Russia manifested the ability to create an industrial system that could rival us, we began suddenly to realize that freedom, competition, self-interest, the Protestant ethic were not essential to the creation of industry. Russia apparently could call upon just as much skill and just as much motivation as the free world. In view of this experience, we came to realize that the physical achievement itself is not the important thing; it is the values which guided men in its for-

mation and the values by which they relate this industrial achievement to the other aspects of social life. It
is true that American businessmen never referred only to the
industrial achievement as their important creation, but to
what they call the "American way of life." But a tendency
always existed to keep the industrial achievement very much in
the foreground with the impression that, if this should ever pass,
the American way of life would pass also. However, if in Russia
a similar industrial achievement could exist without bringing
with it the American way of life, the possibility was suggested
that serious changes in the industrial system might not thereby
mean the end of the American way of life either. The industrial
achievement, in itself, could no longer be used to indicate that
men had been motivated by American values. Something much
more had to be added.

This has served to reinforce the growing awareness that
individualism and freedom must go beyond industrial accomplishments to more important aspects of the culture and society;
and that men must seek to express their values, not only in
their achievements in building industry, but in relating industry
to a much better and more secure way of life for the nation. And
since industry can be related effectively to the community only
through highly complicated organizations, the values of individualism, freedom and competition must express themselves in
forms of group activity, directed toward the good of the community rather than the individual's self-interest.

SUMMARY AND RESOLUTIONS

In summary, I could remark that two things have happened
in American industry: a change in structure; a modification or
redefinition of values. The change in structure is obvious:
from the simple New England farm we have grown to the giant
corporation. From the self-reliant pioneer we have grown to
the sophisticated citizen almost completely dependent for sur-

vival on a complicated mesh of organized activity. The change
in structure was the direct result of the steady, persistent effort
of men to achieve a rational mastery over their environment.
It was the indirect result of man's desire to realize his own potentialities, to fulfill himself by competing for power and rewards
in American business. With the change in structure, and the
changed relationship of this structure to the world, a large number of serious dilemmas have arisen to provoke questions about
American industry, to arouse criticism of it, to compel analysis.
I have not attempted anything approaching a complete analysis.
I was interested only in the effect of certain changes on traditional values.

It is my conviction that the structural changes have compelled Americans and American businessmen to make explicit
the values which before had been confused, taken for granted,
accepted without reflection. Regardless of the strange and
sometimes unreal way in which these values are still expressed
in speeches, statements, advertisements, fundamentlly I am convinced that on a practical level Americans are becoming aware
of the need to express traditional values in quite a different way.
Individual responsibility and effort must now take place in
highly complicated forms of organization prompting the individual to master the techniques and information necessary to
enable him to participate effectively in organized action. Freedom
must be related to the need to conform to those kinds of behavior which will enable the organization to function well for
society. Achievement will be predominantly group achievement,
the work of a community rather than an individual, but group
achievement in which the contribution of gifted people will
play a primary role and be rewarded with high recognition
and prestige.

If we can be as successful in these new manifestations of
American values as we have been in the old, the possibilities of
achievement are extraordinary in the elimination of poverty,

the subordination of nature to man's service, the advancement of level of man's educational and cultural life.

The pressure of self-interest is still great indeed, and the attempt to resort to old manifestations of individualism and freedom within the new environment may still lead to serious harm in our American society. But if men can sufficiently achieve a new expression of American values in the framework of our highly complicated organizations, the American achievement will not have ended, it will have just begun.

William H. Form is Professor of Sociology in in the Department of Sociology and Anthropology, Michigan State University; affiliated with this department since 1947; research associate in the Labor and Industrial Relations Center; research and writing interests in the industrial, occupational and urban areas; his publications include Industrial Sociology *(with D. Miller), 1951;* Community in Disaster *(with S. Nosow), 1957; and* Industry, Labor and Community, *1960.*

William H. Form

TOWARD RE-EVALUATION OF

INDIVIDUALISM IN INDUSTRY

IT IS FORTUNATE THAT FATHER FITZPATRICK FOCUSED ON THE single value, "individualism," rather than on a broad range of values, not only because individualism is so central, but also because the discussion can now have some boundaries. The central question before us is clear: "Can individualism persist as a value in a complex organizational structure which seems antithetical to it?" While acknowledging the dynamic force of individualism in American industry, Father Fitzpatrick realistically suggests that it alone was not responsible for our spectacular industrial achievements. This makes it a value worth defending, one which should be upheld as an end in itself. That is, as a terminal value it should be upheld because it is sacred and not because it has paid off in a material sense. Father Fitzpatrick properly places the discussion of individualism within the context of the greatest issues facing American society today; survival against the threat of an alien ideology, the challenge to meet the yearnings of peoples in technologically underdeveloped areas, and the task of creating meaningful lives domestically while maintaining high standards of living.

As a parenthesis, let me interject that general studies on "values" give me a vague sense of uneasiness because they seem to be far removed from the daily problems which confront common people.[1] I feel that there are three primary reasons for this. The first is that the concept "values" is, as my colleague, C. P. Loomis insists, a broad and spongy one. He suggests that we break it up into constituent elements of ends, norms, and beliefs, and then consider the sentiments in which these elements are clothed.[2] In this discussion, we are primarily concerned with industrial norms. Secondly, studies on values often fail to specify the groups whose norms, ends and beliefs are being analyzed. Most discussions concentrate on the managers and owners of large industry and ignore other occupational groups. Yet recent research suggests that different occupational groups have different norms.[3] Do we *not* need to specify the different norms for the main functional groups in the labor force, such as the corporation managers, small businessmen, labor leaders, governmental officials, professionals, white-collar and manual workers?[4] Third, studies fail to consider negative norms, ends and beliefs for different functional groups.[5] This is especially important for a society such as our own which may be able to achieve consensus only on what it does not want; for example, domination by a foreign ideology. The danger of this negative consensus has been recognized by some as possibly leading to embracing the norms of our foes in the process of resisting them at all costs.

CONTEXTS OF INDIVIDUALISM

To return to the discussion of individualism directly. Future historians may suggest that the era of individualism was a mutant in Western Europe. The era may be labelled finally as an anomic transition from a traditionalistic to an enacted society. Indeed, individualism may be labelled eventually as a

[1] Staley (1952); Bowen (1953); Fitch (1957).
[2] Loomis and Beegle (1957).
[3] Rosenberg (1957).
[4] Form and Miller (1960).
[5] Sjorbert and Cain (1959).

"temporary" entrepreneurial syndrome which never was embraced by the majority of urban workers. It may well be that its loss may be mourned only by small businessmen, managers, and some intellectuals. As Fitzpatrick suggests, the "organizational revolution" hit the workers first and has been moving up the bureaucratic ladder.[6] The employee society finally appears to be including the managers.[7] It may be instructive, in order to understand the future, to examine historically how wage-workers survived the organizational restrictions imposed upon them by individualistic managers. Has the individualism of the workers been eradicated by this or has it been replaced by new norms pushed by emergent organizations such as the labor unions? Can individualism of the managers survive as it becomes engulfed by a bureaucracy of its own making?[8]

THE BASIC QUESTION

The basic question remains: "Can individualism as a norm which arose in a transitional society survive in a new organizational context and still maintain its driving force?" This cannot be easily achieved for two main reasons. First, individualism gets tied into a complex of related norms and is used to justify other sacred norms, such as private enterprise, management prerogatives, union prerogatives, and just plain irresponsibility. Second, individualism has a hollow ring for those who cannot make policy decisions in their economic life — and that may include most of us. A long-term consequence of adhering to norms which may be difficult to realize is that they sooner or later fail to motivate people to provide constructive solutions to workaday problems.[9]

Fortunately, Father Fitzpatrick has suggested two major conditions which may enable individualism to survive. The first is

[6] Boulding (1953).
[7] Drucker (1949).
[8] Gerth and Mills (1942).
[9] Foote (1951).

that the external threat to our society is so great as to enable workers to identify directly with such national purposes as defense, raising the living conditions of underdeveloped countries, and maintaining our own plane of living. Second, the "values of individualism, freedom, and competition must express themselves in forms of group activity, directed toward the good of the community, rather than toward the individual's self-interest."[10] The question seems to be: can the traditional norms of individualism be kept vital by stimulating people to relate their work directly to national purposes, and/or, by stimulating them to identify with national goals through their economic associations, which will, in turn, act responsibly in the face of national threat and goals? Let us appraise the obstacles.

PARTICIPATION IS NOT ENOUGH

Supplying the national defense effort engages only a small proportion of the labor force. Even if the majority could work on defense contracts, prevailing work atmospheres hardly facilitate building a sense of individual contribution to national purpose. Conceivably, businessmen, managers, scientists, and intellectuals working in defense industries can attain a sense of personal contribution. However, the little research evidence available suggests that these very occupations have the most instrumental views of their work and have relatively little ideological sensitivity.[11] Moreover, since they tend to have higher job satisfaction than less skilled workers, they do not need to be concerned with ideologies to make their lives meaningful. Intellectuals in or out of defense industries are, as Mills has pointed out, powerless people who do not participate in decision-making.[12] This is probably just as well, because many of them have horrible ambivalence about national goals and are

[10] Fitzpatrick, in the previous section of this work — end of Part II.
[11] Rosenberg (1957), p. 27.
[12] Mills (1944).

tormented about what the organizational revolution is doing to their shrinking freedom in investigation.

Indirect participation in any national effort, no matter how strenuous, does not seem sufficient to give the worker a meaningful substitute for such a major norm as individualism. Participation is not enough.

> Research has suggested that telling the worker he is an important part of the company, when through *actual* experience he sees he is a very minor part . . . with little responsibility . . . may only increase (his) dissatisfaction. . . . As one worker concluded, "Who do they think they are kidding, us or themselves?" To emphasize to an assembly-line worker that he should feel proud of the four bolts he puts into the right rear end of a car may be viewed by him as an insult. As one employee remarked, "It's ironic — damn. It hurts to know that four bolts are important. What a hell of a life."[13]

This question suggests that participation in any effort, no matter how great, may not be enough. In our society, the question is ubiquitously posed: "Who has the profit, the power, and the glory?" Short of an immanent national catastrophe which threatened everybody, the bulk of employees in large organizations feel a sense of detachment from work. Moreover, outside the plant, the past success we have had in eradicating the pockets of resistance to the "American way of life" may have had the reverse effect from what we wanted: apathy, rather than involvement with national purpose.

The second possibility is that the leaders of the main national economic associations (business, professional, labor and governmental), who share the profit, power and/or glory, may become so infused with national purposes as to stimulate a similar feeling in their subordinates. However, there appears to be no such widespread concern on the part of these directorates. Except for a very few industrial concerns and labor unions,

---

[13] Argyris (1957), p. 154.

the major economic interest groups are following the "traditional individualism" in their operations, i.e. placing economic self-interest above national interest, resisting all governmental control as inherently bad, and displaying suspicion about foreign aid. Indeed, as Berelson may later point out, a content-analysis of the publications of the main functional groups probably reveals very few variations on the traditional theme of unhampered individualism. This may be the time to adopt new norms for a new society.

NEW NORMS FOR A NEW SOCIETY

As suggested, individualism is so disguised in new organizational clothes as to be almost unrecognizable. The most we can hope to rescue from traditional individualism is what may be called "personalism," which is a basic regard for the right of the person to have distinctive beliefs, ends and sentiments. Complex organizations can tolerate a much more personalistic view than they now do. "Personalism" is basic to the "human relations in industry" movement. Of course, an exploitive management may use social science knowledge to work personalism for profit. But it is a chance we must take. In the same way we must accept the organization man, the other-directed person, and the mass society.[14] They are the facts of existence. What many observers miss is that the organization man with his social ethic may be meaningfully involved in his work life, as was the entrepreneur of an earlier era. The semiskilled worker is in a tragic position compared to the Madison Avenue hero — for the worker is apathetic and uninvolved. The frightening thing about the organization man is not his lack of involvement, but his inability to determine his own future without fear.

Fearfully, I propose that a new norm replace traditional individualism, the norm of "multiple-determination." Multiple de-

[14] Whyte (1956).

termination implies that all major economic groups must share in determining all economic and political policies affecting them through a process of collective bargaining. The basic questions are these: Are we willing in economic life to see all occupational groupings consciously organize to define their ends, norms and goals? Are we willing to have all such groups co-determine the policies which affect their common welfare? Are we willing to have collective bargaining infuse the entire bureaucratic structure inside and outside the plant? Can we practice the proper restraints? What a horrible waste of time, to be sure. But it seems to me that multiple determination is a realistic alternative to replace the driving force of the traditional individualism. It may be the only way to build a hierarchy of identifications from the factory floor to the nation.

5

*Values and Religion
in America*

John A. Hutchison has been Professor of Religion,
Columbia University, 1955 to the present; ordained
to the ministry of the Presbyterian Church, 1935;
member of many professional associations,
such as the National Council on Religion in
Higher Education; among his many publications:
We Are Not Divided, *1941;* The Ways of Faith (*with*
J. A. Martin), *1953; editor of* Christian Faith
and Social Action, *1953;* Faith, Reason and Existence,
1955; and The Two Cities, *1957.*

John A. Hutchison

AMERICAN VALUES IN THE

PERSPECTIVE OF FAITH

In this analysis we shall be concerned first with some problems of the theology and philosophy of value, and second with the application of these ideas to the religious situation of American culture today.

THE VALUE LANGUAGE

Implied or presupposed in the contemporary talk about values is an important philosophical and theological assumption which is seldom made explicit and conscious. It is the assumption that human spiritual life can properly and adequately be discussed and described in the language or vocabulary of values. Put it this way: one of the most significant characteristics of the relation of religion to value in our society is this widespread assumption that man's religious life — and indeed his whole spiritual life — can be discussed adequately in these terms. I think this assumption is at least not self-evidently true. Is it the case that we can discuss and describe these aspects of man's life in these terms without hopelessly distorting the subject matter we wish to describe? Is this language appropriate and adequate to its referent?

Before we answer the question with an impatient "Yes, of course, let us get on with the business before us," we may observe that many thoughtful students of the human situation answer in the negative. Among such critics of "value" talk are students of the arts, of ethics, and of religion. They point to the perilous ambiguity of the term "value," to the illicit relativism and subjectivism, and to the vast number of hidden assumptions, often metaphysical and religious assumptions, that hide behind this innocent facade. Again, they point to the ambiguity of "value" or "values," asking if we have here a singular or plural object. Is it "value" or "values" which we seek?

My own situation on Morningside Heights in New York City illustrates in capsule form a few of these problems. In the generally secular and pluralistic intellectual atmosphere of Columbia University, I find the "value" language essential for the discussion of religion with my students and my colleagues. But as I cross Broadway to teach at Union Theological Seminary, I find misgiving and downright hostility among both students and faculty toward the discussion of religion in terms of value. The example of one thoughtful seminary student sticks in my mind, particularly because his conclusion conflicts with mine. In a course on religion and education I had sought to raise the question of whether religion might adequately be discussed in the value-language; and in the final examination I asked students for a discussion of the problem. This student concluded, "No, it is not possible for the Christian to use the value-language. Rather he must say to his secular educational colleague: While we are talking about the same area of human experience, your understanding of it is so different, so incompatible with mine, that communication between us is impossible."

Despite these genuine problems, my solution is to use the "value" language, while being aware of some of its perils. One may construct a kind of lexicon with traditional philosophic and religious terms in one column, and the corresponding terms in value-language in the other column, and thus hope to avoid some of the pitfalls of the new language. But one must use the new language if one is to communicate with many contemporary academic people in the only language they know. There is also a more fundamental reason for using the new language. Despite its shortcomings, it does manage to reassert in terms of contemporary discussion essential elements of traditional religious experience, which in the recent past have been badly misconstrued, or lost sight of.

ULTIMATE VALUATION

Using the value-language, let me address myself to a basic issue, namely, the nature of religious experience. In discussion of human values in the context of social science, religion or religious values are regarded as a special kind of value, which some people take and other people leave alone, which are supposedly characterized by what I can only call a kind of ghostly or spooky supernaturalism, and which are associated professionally with clergymen, with social institutions called churches or synagogues. It is difficult for me to imagine a single cluster of ideas which exhibits more errors and falsehoods than this. Clearly, a fresh start is needed.

Let us attempt such a fresh start, defining religious experience, following Tillich, as "ultimate concern," or as I would like to paraphrase it, as "ultimate valuation." I am using the terms "concern" or "value" interchangeably to designate the motor-affective aspect of personality — that which leads us to act. Literally a value is an object of serious human pursuit; if you chase it, it has value or is a value for you. In saying this, I am not oblivious of Professor Williams' distinction between the object or goal of value and the standard of value. Men do not often pursue an object unless they are persuaded that it conforms with their standards. Whether in fact this persuasion is well-founded may often be questioned. In any case, such attitudes as these — concerns, values, interests, loyalties — are the human raw materials of which religious experience and religions are made.

Now whatever one's brand of psychology, these interests or concerns must be organized into some sort of structure or pattern in a functioning personality. Personality must in some way be unified or integrated. In passing, on the actual playing field of human existence this fact of unification or integration is a religious reality. We do not just blow upon our hands saying, "Go to, now, I will integrate my personality." Rather we find some object of interest or allegiance which claims us, and in the service of this object our lives achieve whatever unity they possess.

Now in the structure or organization of personality (and in the structure and organization of culture, for that matter), certain values achieve top priority. They are the values to which in a pinch a man would sacrifice all else. They are the values which give validity to our other interests or concerns, but which are themselves derived from nothing more fundamental. If I may use a mathematical metaphor, they establish the co-ordinate system or frame of reference for all our valuations. This top priority status is what I mean by "ultimate" as applied to values; any value which has this top priority is ultimate for the person who holds it. It is this which constitutes its ultimacy.

Many questions can be put to this view of ultimate valuation. Is this really the way personality is organized? I have a positivist friend who argues that it is not — that actually the only problem a man faces in organizing his values is similar to that of the juggler who must keep several balls in the air without dropping any one of them. Again, a careful introspective look at the values which claim our interest during the course of a day's life suggests an irreducible plurality of values. This, as Professor J. H. Randall likes to point out, is the element of truth in polytheism. Yet despite this, I am a monotheist. I am so for many reasons, but among them because I believe that the unification of personality is a valid goal.

An ultimate value is, then, a *top priority value;* that is its first trait. In the second place, it is deployed in all of man's existence. Nothing that he does is insignificant for an ultimate value. Perhaps the most obvious illustration of this point is the nature of political allegiance for members of a democratic society and for totalitarians. Most of us have political interests, yet as democrats these interests are limited in character. They exist alongside other interests and are limited by them. And there are surely some parts of our experience to which they do not apply. If we were members of a totalitarian party, neither of these limits would hold. I have never seen a Communist party card, but I am told that the holder promises to guide *all* his activities according to the directives of the party. Now this completely unrestricted use of the term "all" is the clue to the religious or ultimate character of the allegiance which the Communist gives to his party and his movement. Ultimate or religious values are thus total in scope — they embrace *all* of life.

There is a third trait of such values or concerns. They carry with them a unique kind of affective or emotive tone, namely the holy or the sacred. Indeed, I offer it as a definition of the sacred or the holy as a characteristic of human affections, that it is the emotive accompaniment of ultimate valuation or concern. Wherever men commit themselves absolutely or unqualifiedly, there the emotion of the holy or the sacred emerges whether it be attached to the American flag, to the heroes of science, to the statue of alma mater, or to the symbolic objects of a traditional religious faith.

As can be readily seen, there are numerous issues and problems inherent in this characterization of religious experience as ultimate valuation. Let me add two or three comments to guard the flanks of this view and to suggest some of its implications. 1) The experience of ultimate concern or ultimate valuation as it actually occurs — as it happens to us — claims to be objectively oriented. As the experience takes place, the human subject feels himself to be laid hold upon and put in the service of the object. The human aspect of the experience, while certainly free and responsible, claims the character of response to the object. Obviously, this claim must be critically appraised and evaluated. This appraisal is surely part of the work of theology and philosophy. The term "object of ultimate concern or valuation" is a good secular paraphrase for "deity" as that term might be used in natural theology.

2) Now the various historic faiths or religions of mankind — Christianity, Judaism, Buddhism — and the faith-substitutes, such as Marxism or secular humanism, can be regarded as specific ways in which ultimate concern is articulated and understood. They are ways in which men have understood, expressed, and lived out this basic aspect of their existence. Ultimate concern or valuation is the human stuff of which religions are made. What each religion does is to take this material of human allegiance or loyalty and work it up in its own distinctive way.

3) It also follows from this view that there are no religious values as a special class of values. There are only fundamental human values seen under the aspect of God or the object of ultimate concern. Now if this view of religion is at all correct, we must fundamentally revise the relation of religion to personality and its values, and to culture and its values. We must give up the view of religious values as a special kind of value apart from other human values. Rather ultimate or religious values stand at the creative center of personality and culture. (The converse is also true; the values which stand at the center of personality and culture constitute the actual, working religion of the person or culture.) As such they are not so much ultimate values as they are primal values. In the language of traditional religion, they constitute the faith by which the man or the culture lives. From this vital center other human values are created, sustained, and renewed. Once in existence these values are the

ingredients of both personality and culture. Brought to sharp focus these values *are* religious faith; deployed in the whole life of individuals and societies, they are the constitutive ingredients of personality and culture. There is thus a reciprocal relation between religion on the one hand, and personality and culture on the other.

Religions may thus be viewed and studied as systems of value creation and maintenance, support and organization. Conversely, values may be regarded as the products or by-products of faith. This assertion is not offered for uncritical acceptance but as an agenda for study — for a kind of study of fundamental human values which will involve co-operative inquiry on the part of social scientists on the one hand, and philosophers and theologians on the other hand. Such a project of study might have the incidental advantage of bringing these groups of scholars back into communication with each other, after years and decades of mutual suspicion and alienation.

AMERICAN RELIGIOUS VALUES

Let us now try to apply the ideas we have been elaborating to the analysis of contemporary American values. We cannot undertake anything like systematic analysis. Rather what we will do is what oil geologists call test-boring into the soil of American culture at certain points. First, we will make some observations about the contemporary upsurge of religious interest in America, and second, we will extend these comments to embrace certain more general traits of our culture. In all of this, I will simply assume without offering proof or evidence that the Judeo-Christian or biblical tradition of religion is a crucially important aspect of the Western cultural tradition, and hence of that part of the West which we call America. To say that there is a Judeo-Christian or biblical ingredient in American values and valuation is of course to say something more pervasive than an assertion about overt religious allegiance or affiliation in America. It is so because of this Judeo-Christian element in our culture. Put this assertion in extreme form. The veriest atheist or agnostic in our midst entertains certain valuations, he responds this way and not that way because of events long ago and far away in the land of Palestine — much as this atheist or agnostic may deny or ignore this aspect of his values.

Now turning to the current upsurge of religious interest in American culture, to our so-called return to religion, let us look at this social phenomenon in the light of the assumptions about religion and value we have been developing. The return to religion is a large and significant social phenomenon. Whether it is equally significant religiously seems questionable. First, as to the magnitude and significance of this phenomenon, let me refer briefly to Will Herberg's book, *Protestant, Catholic and Jew,* in which the author points out many of the important indices of institutional religious activity which have turned very sharply up during the past decade or two. About 95 per cent of Americans claimed some religious preference in the first half of the sixth decade of the twentieth century, clearly an all-time high. Regarding actual church membership, similar increases both in absolute numbers and a percentages of population may be cited. In 1950 membership in organized religious bodies stood at 85,000,000 people, or about 57 per cent of the population. In 1953 this percentage was up to 59.5 per cent. According to the *Yearbook of American Churches* it grew to 62 per cent by 1956. The same source indicates that the figures dipped slightly in the year 1957, down to 61 per cent.

Apparently, then, Americans in numbers and proportions of the population unparalleled in previous history have been swarming into churches and synagogues.

I know these figures have recently been challenged by other sociologists, among them Seymour Lipset of the University of California, writing in the *Columbia University Forum.* We cannot pause to offer detailed analysis of his criticisms except to state his contentions that the figures are not reliable, and that the religious quality of this upsurge is not very high. With the second assertion I agree, but with the first I disagree. Other figures, independent of the *Yearbook of American Churches,* tend to substantiate the figures. The census sample of two years ago put the figures even higher. And recently a group of sociologists in the Protestant Council of New York arrived at a figure of 65 per cent religious membership for the population of Greater New York, an area not usually regarded as the most religious section of America. This 65 per cent was divided 29 per cent Roman Catholic, 19 per cent Protestant, and 17 per cent Jewish. The conclusion I draw from these figures is that factually the return to religion is a very large social phenomenon which thus claims more detailed study from social scientists than it has so far received.

As to our understanding of this phenomenon, let me briefly call attention to Herberg's work again. It has been attacked, but I have yet to see a well-reasoned refutation of it. Herberg begins with the early or mid-19th century structure of American culture. It was a dominantly Protestant culture, with a small Roman Catholic minority and an even smaller Jewish minority. Changes came in the form of successive waves of immigration to America between mid-19th and early 20th century. Indeed it is not too much to assert with Hansen that "America is immigrants." Thus it follows that the immigrant's state of mind is of crucial importance to the American culture pattern.

Herberg has sought to study this state of mind with the tools of depth psychology. He observes that the first-generation immigrant is a stranger in an alien land, and consequently he clings anxiously to the folkways of the old country. By contrast, his son, the second generation, in the new country seeks to forget these foreign traces and to Americanize as rapidly as possible. But *his* son in turn, the third generation, has a still dif-

ferent viewpoint. He has no frenzied or anxious desire to establish his American-ness, for he *is* securely American. Rather his
problem is a different, indeed an opposite one, namely how he
will establish his identity and location in the large and be-
wildering cultural community of America. In what concrete
cultural terms will he express his American-ness? Often he does
so by recovering precisely some of the cultural traits which his
father sought to forget. As the historian, Hansen, has put the
matter, what the second generation seeks to forget, the third
generation seeks to remember.

Yet which of these persistent cultural traits will the third
generation lay hold upon to establish its identity in the larger
community of American culture? For many of the traits of the
old country have fallen away and perished as the successive waves
of immigrants have made their place in American society. However, one trait, namely religious affiliation, has not thus perished,
but has persisted.

It is a sociologically demonstrable fact that religious identity
in the three main American religious traditions has persisted.
It is precisely this factor which has provided a way by which
many Americans establish their identity and location in American society. It is, according to Herberg, this social use of religion which in large measure accounts for its present upsurge in
American society. The three main religious traditions, Catholicism, Protestantism, and Judaism, are regarded as ways of
expressing American-ness, of locating an individual in American
society.

To be sure, we must carefully avoid any one-cause explana-
tions of large and complex social phenomenon. So here there
are many other contributing factors which importantly condition the result. We may observe in the return to religion factors
as various as the sense of inadequacy of the whole modern view
of man and the search for an adequate view, as illustrated again
by men as different as Thomas Merton and Reinhold Niebuhr;

or on the other end of the spectrum, we may observe the cult of positive thinking peddling its narcotics in the age of anxiety. But the large fact described by Herberg sets the context in which these many other factors operate.

Now the use of biblical religion — whether in its Catholic, Protestant, or Jewish form — as a way of expressing Americanness involves a subtle (and sometimes an unsubtle) degradation of biblical religion. What is taking place in our midst is the growth of a new American civic religion which employs the traditional language and symbols of Judaism and Christianity. Here is a situation where if we get behind the traditional religious labels and professions to the value-structure which is the heart of the religious experience, we find some real conflicts. We use Christian labels, but they stand for new and different realities. We still say "God," but our object of ultimate concern or valuation is construed in exclusively American terms. I have listened to sermons in Christian churches or Jewish synagogues where the value-structure seemed to me to be very similar to that of state Shinto in Japan or to Caesar worship in ancient Rome. In other words, the religion to which we are returning is a species of American tribalism or nationalism. Such an American nationalism is no more compatible with the biblical God than is any other species of exclusive nationalism or tribalism.

Now let us briefly add two further comments on the current American religious upsurge. Unlike some religious revivals in human history, it seems singularly devoid of the fruits of faith; and this is so, largely because it is a phenomenon not so much of faith as of the lack or absence of faith. When we look historically at some religious revivals or renewals in human development we see authentic value-creation, which is what we would be led to expect from the hypothesis of the first part of this paper. Looking, for example, at our own American history, the Great Awakening of the 1730's and 1740's bore fruit in educational activity, in the impulse to social reform in ways ranging from temperance to abolition. Or look at the impact of ancient Christianity upon the Greco-Roman world into which it first came. Even as unsympathetic an observer as Gibbon concedes a whole range of new values, such as a new sense of human dignity among the lower classes of society, which were the by-products of Christianity's early victory in the Roman world. Looking to the Orient, we see that the impact of Buddhism upon the society of ancient India led to many new values — ethical, intellectual, and esthetic. Similar results accrued from the impact of Buddhism upon the culture of Japan. Apparently creative and vital religion always makes a difference in the values which a people or a person holds. Of religions the biblical injunction seems to hold: "By their fruits ye shall know them."

How does the current American religious revival look from this viewpoint? It is admittedly too early to make any safe and settled judgments; and I am sure that in all this large movement there is some creative religion, some religion that does make a difference, but it consists of small minority groups, small spots of vitality amid a larger situation which is, taken as a whole, singularly barren of results of any sort. Our churches are full; we are annually building more and more of them, but the sad fact is that they don't seem to make much difference. This came home to me with particular force after Billy Graham's campaign in New York. He spoke to packed meetings at Madison Square Garden for several weeks, but when it was all over there were no detectable results or consequences in the common life of New York. The same social and civic problems remained, the same issues confront us now as before Mr. Graham spoke and worked in our midst. This seems to me broadly true of the whole upsurge of religious interest. It has borne very little fruit; it just hasn't made much difference in the values of individual Americans or of our culture generally. Thus it is like the barren fig tree which elicited so negative a comment from Christ.

If we ask why this should be, why a religious upsurge which judged externally and objectively is doing so well is actually so devoid of the results which we may fairly expect from a living faith, the answer is ready at hand. America has rushed pell-mell into church not out of any genuine sense of religious faith or conviction, but rather out of a growing anxiety which arises from a lack of faith. Faith in the biblical sense, *emunah* in the Hebrew of the Old Testament and *pistis* in the Greek of the New Testament, is an attitude of conviction and trust which gives a man inner certitude and an inner source from which all his outer values proceed.

Now there is a good deal of evidence that it is precisely this inner center of certitude that has been lacking, and lacking this our return to church has been very largely motivated by the desire to play it safe. It is like the story of the man on his deathbed who, asked by the attending clergyman if he would renounce the devil and all his works, replied, "In my situation I am not in a position to offend anyone." As a nation we have gone back to church with just this spirit. Lacking any fundamental convictions, we simply don't want to offend anyone, least of all any gods that might be. Lacking any deep or burning convictions, we have decided to take out a kind of fire insurance policy.

It is, in short, because we are so self-centered, so self-enclosed, that our religious revival has been so hollow and so uncreative. Indeed, one can adduce the most excellent reasons, both theological and psychological, why this unfortunately negative and depressing result should obtain. With this motivation it is precisely what we should expect. Since when has self-centeredness been a virtue and not a paralyzing vice?

Now let us extend this observation in two ways, first to take in the nonchurchgoing members of American culture, and second to include other relations than ostensibly religious ones. The other-directed man and the organization man are often observed and important characters in politics, economics and other fields, as well as religion. One suspects that Everyman has become other-directed and organization-minded in our contemporary American society.

Here we may relate these tendencies to the motivation we have already sketched for American religion. If a person has no deep or vital convictions there is a kind of expedient prudence in playing safe. If he has no deep inner convictions from which to live, there is a worldly kind of wisdom in playing along with whatever powers appear to be in control of the situation. So Everyman in the sixth decade of 20th-century America, having abjured all absolutes, having nothing for which he would literally stake his life, is left with the alternative of fitting himself in, adjusting himself or conforming to his cultural context. He is a decent, moderately public-spirited citizen, a family man, and a churchman. If with T. S. Eliot we call him a hollow man, we must add that he seems well-adjusted to the hollowness.

But history has played a very dirty trick on this contemporary American. It has conspired situations, political, economic, social, and religious in which he must make all-out decisions. And this is the one thing under heaven he is unprepared and unqualified to do. He hasn't the resources of faith to make these decisions. His personality is ill-equipped to stand this kind of strain, and the greater strain of living a whole life poised on one brink or another. He talks a lot about courage, steadiness and poise, but his heart trouble and his peptic ulcers belie his words. What the future holds for this man — if in nuclear fate or providence he is spared for a future — lies beyond the scope of this analysis. The point is that now, for the time being, here he rather indecisively stands.

Joseph H. Fichter, S.J. has been Professor and Chairman of the Department of Sociology, Loyola University, New Orleans, 1947 to the present; member of many professional societies and active in organizations such as the National Urban League; writing and research are extensive; among which are Roots of Change, 1939; Social Relations in the Urban Parish, 1957; Sociology, 1957; Parochial School, 1958; and Religion as an Occupation: A Study in the Sociology of Professions, 1961.

Joseph H. Fichter, S.J.

RELIGIOUS VALUES,

A SOCIOLOGICAL PERSPECTIVE

DR. HUTCHISON PRESENTS TWO GENERAL PROBLEMS IN HIS analysis, each of which is worthy of deep and separate consideration. The first is an attempt to define religious experience in the terminology of values; and the second is the suggestion that the present upsurge of religion in America is somehow a spurious cultural product, rather than a biblical-religious phenomenon. It seems to me that the conclusions concerning the second problem flow from the manner in which the first problem is defined.

If religion is defined as "ultimate concern," or as "religious experience," it tends to remain in the realm of the personal and the psychological. Even though Tillich's explanation of ultimacy is added to this definition so that religion has "top priority" in the value-system of the individual, and has "relevance to all of experience" in which he may be involved, the concept of religion still remains rooted in the individual.[1] This focus upon personal experience prevents an understanding of the cultural aspect of religion; and it is no wonder that it leads to an interpretation of religion in America as "merely" a cultural phenomenon.

---

[1] "Religion may be described as the answer given to these questions — the answer to the questions, Whence, Whither, and Why? More formally, religion may be described as the ultimate meaning of man's existence." John A. Hutchison (1956), p. 25.

The sociologist approaches religion from another point of view and finds another definition closer to the realities of religion. In this conceptual framework, religion is a relationship with God and with fellow men.[2] It is a network of patterns, roles and relations that have become institutionalized so that men implement their relation with God in and through each other. It is social experience that comes under scrutiny, and as in every other human institution this experience is normatively guided by the shared values of the people. It may be said in passing that even one's personal relation with God is largely a learned social product, and that it both affects and is affected by the culture in which it exists.

RELIGION IN AMERICAN CULTURE

Dr. Hutchison seems to agree with Will Herberg's thesis that religion in America is an earth-bound culture-religion rather than a genuine transcendental phenomenon.[3] There are various ways in which this distinction can be understood, but there is one misinterpretation of culture-religion that requires attention at this point. People seem to think that they are making a stricture against religion when they call it "sociological." The fact is, of course, that religion cannot be properly understood if it is wrenched from the culture and the society in which it is practiced. It would be a surprise if religion were not sociological and cultural, if it were completely out of tune with the culture in which it exists.

Religion is the cultural property of all societies, and no

---

[2] "Among all groups, religious activity is a deliberate attempt to get into helpful relationship with powers, personalized or impersonal, that are believed to control the unknowns of human life. People conduct most of the activities jointly." Joyce O. Hertzler (1954), p. 203.

[3] Will Herberg (1955), chap. XI, looks at "Religion in America in the Perspective of Faith," and anticipates the general theme of Professor Hutchison, who looks at "American Values in the Perspective of Faith."

historical or contemporary society has ever been without some form of religion. Whatever the supernatural ingredients, the forms of religious beliefs and the rituals of religious observances are part of the social heritage because they are products of the group.[4] The fact that organized religious bodies convey, promote, and often originate values, makes the Church an important influence on society. Organized religion, by its very mission, must "interfere" with the total society, and this interference is obviously on the level of what social scientists call values.

There has been much talk about the Protestant ethic in this set of discussions. We have also heard much discussion on the definition of values. The fact that Protestantism has influenced the ways of thinking and behavior in our economic ethical system is clear evidence of the relationship between religion and values. This indicates too that values are the "things that matter," what people believe in strongly enough to live by, fight for, even die for. A social value is that which people think "worthwhile"; they treasure it, they object to its desecration.[5] Kolb points out that sociologists generally have focused on values as norms and rules, rather than as objects. "From this definition of value as objects meaningful to subjects, combined with the emphasis on rules as the values important for sociologists, the meaning of the value-concept for sociologists has gradually shifted, so that the element of *normativeness* characteristic of rules has become the determining criterion rather than the element of objectivity."[6]

An emphasis on values as merely subjective attitudes towards the rules of behavior, or a contrasting emphasis on values as highly important objects that act as criteria of behavior, will

[4] See the analysis on this point of John A. Hutchison (1956), chap. VII, "Religion and Culture," pp. 203-31.

[5] See the clear and practical explanation of values in Robin M. Williams (1952), chap. XI.

[6] William L. Kolb, in Howard Becker and Alvin Boskoff (1957).

probably have significant consequences on the observer's total approach to sociocultural realities. As Howard Becker says, "values are inescapable," and "conduct is always normative."[7] It seems important to note that people in society have a two-fold appreciation of values, one toward the object of value itself and one toward the capacity of the object to satisfy social needs; but these two aspects fold into one and can be separated only for purposes of analytical clarity.[8] This concept of values is clearly broader than, and includes more than, the religious values in the culture. Religious values affect other institutionalized values, and are affected by them.

It is frequently asserted that the values of religion are the "highest" in any society. They are the holy values dealing with holy entities, and are therefore on a level above profane values. They call for the most profound respect on the part of the individual, and they are surrounded by solemn rituals which set them apart. These religious values may be extremely important in both the so-called secular and the so-called sacred types of society, but in the profane society they are likely to be only surreptitiously significant, or to be downgraded from the holy and supernatural level to the kind of nationalistic or "culture-religion" level of which Herberg speaks.[9]

One of the central problems in a discussion of values is the confusion of the secular and the profane types of society. The literature of sociology is sprinkled with dichotomous typologies that have not always helped to unravel this confusion: Durkheim's mechanical-organic, Toennies' *Gemeinschaft-Gesellschaft*, Mayo's established-adaptive, Toynbee's Yin-state and Yang-state, Parsons' particularistic-universalistic, and many others. All of them stress the relatively unchanging isolated character of the

[7] Howard Becker (1950), pp. 6-18.
[8] Joseph H. Fichter (1957), chap. XIII, "Values."
[9] This terminology of sacred-secular and holy-profane follows the analysis of Becker (1950), pp. 249 ff.

sacred type and the dynamic, accessible aspect of the secular type. "A society that incorporates and sustains an impermeable value-system is sacred; one that embodies a permeable value-system is secular."[10] The difficulty in the discussions of the present meeting seems to lie in the assumption that the secular American society must necessarily be opposed to, or at least is only reluctantly prepared to accept, the values of a holy and supernatural religion.

There can be no question — in a technical sociological terminology — that the American society is secular; nor is this the question with which we are here concerned. The value-system of the American culture *includes* religious values in which there is a genuine "trust in God" even though the motivational attitude for this trust may often be utilitarian. But has there ever existed a culture in which this practical motivation for a religious orientation did not occur? The point of importance here is the fact that while the American value-system is secular, it is by no means profane. Dr. Hutchison, among other critics of religion in America, seems to feel that a "profanation" of religion is going on apace because of hedonism, lack of faith, absence of the fruits of faith, the use of religion for ulterior purposes, a development of organization-mindedness, and many other contemporary characteristics.

NEW DIRECTIONS IN RELIGION

I have suggested in another place that the present upsurge of religious affiliation and practice is a trend in another direction.

What seems to be happening in this area of common values is that a quasi-nationalism has developed to replace deep-rooted ethnic and immigrant allegiances of a former generation. As the population moves further from its immigrant origins the people focus more on what are assumed

[10] *Ibid.,* p. 253; but see the three charts on the typologies of society, pp. 258-60.

to be the "highest" American values. This suggests that a kind of nationalism, by substituting for the former loyalties of ethnic groups, has also managed to supersede any system of unifying religious beliefs, and has allowed for fundamental differences of religious beliefs because the latter are no longer considered important. If this description is valid, we have returned (but from the opposite direction) to the kind of thing that happened when the rise of national states in Europe replaced the United Christendom of the Middle Ages.[11]

In all fairness, however, to the truly religious (in the sense of holy and supernatural) development of America today, this analysis must go a step further. It seems to me that the cult of the "American way of life" as a quasi-nationalistic "culture religion" had begun to recede even before Herberg proposed it as a thesis. The contemporary religious revival appears to be groping for something more genuine than this "way of life" in which even the core of common values, highly estimable and ennobling as they are, does not satisfy the social needs of the people. "The subsidiary ethnic groups that used to preserve adherence are no longer functioning satisfactorily. It may well be that Americans are now becoming loyal to religious values in a way in which they used to be loyal to their ethnic values."[12]

What we are facing here is a problem of cultural interpretation. We are holding on to a traditional concept of religion that has been weighted down — in the accidents of history — with cultural, mainly European, characteristics. Alongside this, we hold a concept of the American culture, chock-full of values that are "non-religious," like the rational, pragmatic, optimistic approach to life, the importance of progress, meaningful work and individual achievement.[13]

---

[11] Joseph H. Fichter (1958).
[12] *Ibid.*, p. 369.
[13] For a few comments on common American values, see Joseph H. Fichter (1957), pp. 308-310; John Cuber (1956), pp. 486-87; Williams (1951), pp. 388-422.

Since culture is a complex of institutions, religion must be functionally distinguished from the other major institutions. Thus, like every major institution, religion can be identified by its cultural characteristics and can be an influence upon the culture. This elementary observation makes it clear that while religion becomes Americanized culturally there still remain value-conflicts between the religious and other institutions. In this imperfect world there remains much antisocial conduct upon which the Church frowns. The forces of Mammon and the forces of God are not planning a summit meeting, nor is there any hope even of an armistice. This conflict of values does not mean that the Incarnation was a mistake or that religion cannot be "incarnated" into a culture.[14]

Genuine "biblical" religion shared certain characteristics with other institutions in the United States. The aspects of religion which seem most highly evaluated by Americans are those which are personal, pragmatic, optimistic and tolerant. This is another way of saying that some of the major value-orientations of the total American culture are also those of its religious institution.[15] It must be remembered, however, that these characteristics indicate emphases; they do not eradicate opposite characteristics. Indeed, to many people it is a paradox that religion is both personal and social, that the pragmatic person can do "foolish" things for God, that optimism is tempered by the realities of sin and tragedy, that tolerance draws the line at evil and error.

[14] The tension between Christianity and the world, as Professor O'Dea calls it, requires an answer to the question whether the world is really important in the divine scheme of salvation, or whether it is so "dangerous" that we must both renounce and denounce it. See Thomas O'Dea (1959), pp. 96-109.

[15] This can be said even though Williams firmly asserts that "American religious organizations are extraordinarily segregated from other institutionalized structures . . . the very fact that religion in our culture is so frequently equated with the churches is a telling indication of the compartmentalization of religious norms." See Williams (1951), p. 339.

Some Americans seem to be embarrassed by the growth of piety and religious devotion in America. They accept the criticism of some European observers concerning our "materialism," and make public confession of our lack of "deep-rooted faith." There is often a kind of global contrast made between the spirituality of the East and the materialism of the West, between the faithful millions of Asia and the faithless millions of America. To my mind this is a misinterpretation of major proportions.[16] The notion that spirituality flourishes in hungry poverty and that infidelity flourishes in material prosperity is an easily demonstrable error.

It is an oddity if Americans are humble about nothing in the culture except the religious institution. The faith that Americans have in each other is not limited only to nonreligious groups, and in the religious groups it is not limited only to faith in man.[17] The so-called materialism of Americans is offset by their generosity, humanitarianism, sympathy for the underdog, in social movements that have raised the status and the aspirations of all minority groups in the population. There is no need to apologize for our typical American social virtues, or to suppose that these virtues simply cannot be spiritually and religiously motivated.

[16] Interestingly enough, the most-quoted commenators on American life, like de Tocqueville, Bryce, Siegfried and Myrdal, do not make this misinterpretation, but speak of the high moral and religious level of American behavior. "America believes in and aspires to something much higher than its plane of actual life." Gunnar Myrdal (1944), p. 21.

[17] Indeed, Hutchison remarks that "the real nature of faith is illustrated by the relation of persons in community. The pattern or structure of any man's conduct is just such a pattern of trusts or assumptions." See Hutchison (1956), p. 107.

6

Values and

Mass Communications

in America

*Bernard Berelson has been Professor and
Director of the Bureau of Applied Social
Research, Columbia University, since 1959;
president of the American Association
of Public Opinion Research, 1951-1952; special analyst,
Foreign Broadcast Intelligence Service FCC, 1941-1944;
professor of Graduate Library School and Division of the
Social Sciences, University of Chicago, 1946-1951; director of
the Behavioral Science Program of the Ford Foundation,
1951-1957; professor in the Graduate School of Business,
University of Chicago, 1957-1959; active in many
organizations and author of a number of
publications, including:* The People's Choice
(*with others*), *1948;* Content Analysis, *1952;*
Voting (*with others*), *1954;* Graduate Education
in the United States, *1960.*

Bernard Berelson

THE GREAT DEBATE ON

CULTURAL DEMOCRACY*

As I began the preparation of this paper, I soon found myself at a crossroad. I could have presented to you a detailed, footnoted account of what the social scientists know, or think they know, about the effect of communications upon values: what usually passes as a scholarly review of the literature. For good or ill, I decided not to take that low road, however well-mapped and lighted and smooth it is, thanks to the heavy academic traffic. Instead, I chose the high road — the opportunity presented by this occasion, and even the responsibility, to raise some Big Questions about mass communication and American values. This road, as you will soon see, is full of bumps, twists, and dark spots, but if we persevere, it is more likely in the end to lead us where we want to go.

The important issues involved in this topic are best put in the form of a debate, the debate, if you will, on the problems and prospects of cultural democracy. The debate on political democracy was sharpened almost 200 years ago by the need to shape the new state, and again 100 years ago by the need to preserve it. The debate on educational democracy was at its

* I am indebted to Henry Murray, whose use of the conversational form in his essay on "Individuality" in *The American Style* first gave me the idea of trying it here; and to William McPhee, who provided both encouragement and advice on the use of the form when I most needed them.

height 75 years ago, with the rise of popular schooling; and the debate on what might be termed economic democracy about 25 years ago, with the rise of the New Deal and the welfare state. Those debates have set the background. Our political forms are settled, and they give the mass of the people a clear and strong say in how things should be, even in cultural matters. The educational revolution has provided a higher and higher level of mass literacy and the economic revolution has provided more and more leisure. Into this situation, within the space of our own lifetimes, have come the movies, massive circulation of the national magazines, paperback books, network radio, and, only yesterday, television.

Small wonder then, that these are, and should be, the years of the great debate on cultural democracy: how well does the system of mass communication serve the cultivation of cultural values in America, in the broadest sense? Are the mass media degrading modern man with an alluring and seductive diet of *kitsch,* or are the media as good as modern man deserves or can take? Should the media give the public what it wants, on democratic grounds, or should they give the public what someone thinks is good for the public, on ethical and artistic grounds? Should the media force people to a serious consideration of life's purposes, or should they facilitate an escape from life? Should the media force people toward an uncongenial position of self-inquiry, or should they support and strengthen existing beliefs?

The trouble with the debate, as currently carried on, is that it is seldom joined. The major points of view are seldom confronted with one another's arguments, so the debate does not seem to move ahead. The intellectuals attack popular culture in the little magazines and in the academies. The men of action defend themselves on Madison Avenue. And the students of the subject, the social scientists, report their researches in terms uncongenial to the core of the debate, if not downright unreadable by the other debaters.

Suppose these three camps were forced to a confrontation of positions? That is what I have attempted to do here — to put their main arguments down in such juxtaposition that they are compelled to deal with one another's strong points as well as their own weak ones. For this purpose, I have three spokesmen — Academicus, Practicus, and Empiricus. After they have debated the matter, I reserve the right to return for the last words and the drawing of morals.

Academicus: I propose that we inquire into what we know about the effect of mass communications upon values and the way American values are reflected in mass communications; and that we then raise some issues of an ethical or even philosophical nature about the influence of the mass media in modern life. I know that social scientists pretend to deal with the facts and nothing but the facts, yet they must occasionally transcend their narrow professional boundaries in order to deal with some important issues and problems that cannot be solved or even recognized within their reservations. The Big Questions about values aren't simply matters of fact, though I'm willing to start there in order to fill in the background. Do the mass media influence values in the United States?

Empiricus: That is an easy question and you get an easy answer: Yes. But like most questions that permit a yes-or-no answer on a complex matter, it is hardly worth answering. But if the question is, *"How* do the mass media influence values?" it becomes more useful, more interesting, and at the same time more difficult to answer. Let me try to say quickly what seems to me worth saying, as the outcome of what passes for scientific investigation of the matter.

To start with, perhaps the most central generalization in the inventory of mass communication studies is simply this: the nature of the audience — its social position, educational status, interests, attitudes, and beliefs — largely determines first what communications will be seen or heard; then, how they will be perceived and interpreted; and finally, what effect they will have. And the more strongly people feel about something — that is, the more valuable it is for them — the less their behavior will be subject to outside stimuli like those provided by the media. The less likely they will be to see or hear uncongenial communications, the less credibility they will assign to them when seen or heard, and the less they will accept them, even as something to be taken into account.

Academicus: That's the trouble with you social scientists: when you do say something that the rest of us can understand, it turns out to be an obviousity inside a platitude wrapped in a tautology. All I hear you saying is that man's values, which by definition are strongly-held beliefs, are not subject to every wind of doctrine blown across the eyes or ears by the managers of the mass media.

Empiricus: That is about all I have said thus far. I said "simply this" because it is simple, but like so many other simple things, it is usually overlooked, forgotten, or neglected — especially in its implications for Big Issues like the one we are discussing. For example, at some point soon you are going to declaim about the terribly debasing influence of the media upon our taste, our morals, and our values, and I thought I ought to forestall that equally obvious and trite attack of the intellectuals by stressing the limited nature of the media's effect upon the society.

Academicus: Just one moment. You haven't really found that the media have "limited effect on society." All you have found, apparently, is that they have a limited effect on strongly-held beliefs, which is something else again. Why, you even imply the converse, that they do influence weakly-held positions: and that is just the point. The problem of the times is precisely this: that the heterogeneity of American society and the rapid social changes that science and technology are bringing have made our values unclear, uncertain, weak, and transitory. More adjustment is apparently winning the day; in the absence of clear standards of judgment, we adjust to whatever is held out to us as the model and call that our value.

At the same time that values have been weakening, however, our capacity to control man is increasing through the systematic effort of the sciences and through the pervasiveness and the persuasiveness of the media. In an unpublished memorandum, my friend Robert Morison has put the matter in a stimulating way:

> The ethical question is really one of deciding how far society can allow any person or group to use any effective method for controlling other people's behavior. . . . Obviously, an orderly social, political, and economic life is simply impossible if some means are not used to insure that the great mass of people behave in a reasonably consistent and cooperative manner. A variety of means, all of which may be subsumed under the term 'persuasive,' are employed for this purpose. . . . So long as the methods used in appealing to the passions were largely a matter of intuition and empirical trial and error, the situation was not so bad. Men of independent mind could remain reasonably free simply because their knowledge of themselves was approximately equal to the knowledge and skill of those who wish to control them. Now, however, the situation is changing rapidly. Knowledge of human behavior is becoming organized and accumulative. In a word, it is becoming scientific. That is not to say that the behavioral sciences are as yet to be regarded as fully qualified members of the scientific community. . . . But it is not too early to prepare ourselves for the day when there will be a behavioral science which will make possible the control of human behavior with a high degree of precision.

> Already there is enough organized knowledge available so that advertising men can make most people want things they never wanted before. Not only this, but there is a highly developed apparatus for testing various different methods of persuasion so that ineffective ones may be rapidly abandoned and more subtly effective ones put in their place. . . .

> We are coming to recognize that organized knowledge puts
> an immense amount of power in the hands of the people
> who take the trouble to master it. . . . It is clear on the
> record that such people have the power to take over our
> society, but absolutely no responsibility, expressed or im-
> plied, to determine its direction.

Hence the problem: we have greater power to control man,
but less knowledge of what to control him for. At the same time
that we become more skilled and proficient as to means, we
have ironically become more uncertain and doubtful as to ends.
And the communication media are right in the center of the
problem: they *are* capable of influencing us when we don't know
what to want ourselves — just as you said.

Empiricus: That is an intriguing and dramatic formulation — too dramatic, I'm afraid. The media just aren't that
powerful, not even on the things that don't matter, like what
kind of cornflakes or toothpaste you buy. I know several advertising men who *wish* they could "make most people want
things they never wanted before" but none who think they can.
As for the important things, their power is still less — except
as background and in the very long run.

Hence, a state of affairs that has always been considered bad
turns out in this context to be a good thing indeed. That is
the fact with which we began, namely, that people tend to see
only what they want to see, to interpret what the media tell
them only in line with their own feeling, and to accept and
reject messages as they like. People have typically considered
such self-selection of communication materials as you did and
as I have too, as evidence of prejudice, bias, lack of objectivity,
lack of reasonableness, and just plain stubbornness. But seen
in the context of the power to control man, it becomes a saving
grace in the whole situation.

Across from the title page of their clever book *Movies,*
Wolfenstein and Leites quote a few lines from James Thomson:

> But when a dream, night after night, is brought

Throughout a week, and such weeks few or many
Recur each year for several years, can any
Discern the dream from real life in aught?

The rhetorical answer, of course, is "no." But the real answer
is "yes" — or at least "yes" to a very large degree. It is precisely
here, I would claim, that the findings of the behavioral sciences
on the short-range invulnerability of people's values through
the influence of the communication media carry important
philosophical implications. The influence of the media is greatest
where it does not matter: in affecting superficial actions like
what kind of face soap to use or in channelling lightly-held attitudes. But in anything that really does matter — nationalism,
religion, values of individualism or ambition, positions connected with class or ethnic status — on these the media almost
never score. To establish a national product may not take long,
but it does to establish a national image or idea.

Practicus: I'm afraid I must register an objection to fellows
like Empiricus who have made a career out of debunking the
power of the mass media. We need to debunk the debunkers.
I know the studies to which you refer, and none of them ever
observed people for more than a few months at a time. Even
a national advertiser has to keep his message going for years
before he notices effects, and if you are concerned with values,
then you should be thinking of generations instead of months.
In such terms, the media may very well be quite effective — as
you said, in the long run.

Academicus: Here I must agree with Practicus. The present
tendencies toward adjustment and other-directedness, toward
what has been called fun morality, toward interest in personality
rather than character, toward superficiality and thinness in
personal relations — such tendencies may very well have been
accelerated and reinforced by the media.

Empiricus: Perhaps. But you asked me to tell you what we
do know, and on that basis, so far, we have not verified any

results that would justify Academicus' fears or Practicus' claims. We would have to say that both are exaggerated. Let me continue with some of the reasons. It is true that in matters where values are weak or ambiguous, the media do exercise more influence — *if* they can get people's attention in the first place. We like to say that people's values are anchored in their group attachments — change their groups, or the situations in which their group lives, and you change their values, but not in other ways, at least not much for settled adults. The media themselves can't do much to change even political attitudes, or feelings about Negroes or Jews, let alone basic values. But for people torn between conflicting group attachments or for those with weak attachments — who are often, and paradoxically, referred to as the nonpartisans or the uncommitted or even the independents — the unhappy fact is that they pay very little attention. So the media are faced with a situation in which those who do read or listen cannot readily be swayed due to strong conviction whereas those who could be swayed cannot be reached due to weak interest.

Academicus: But precisely my complaint about the mass media arises from the fact that they occupy the center of attention in America. As you fellows are the first to know, television itself gets more hours of attention each week than anything but home and work, and perhaps it rivals them. You can't get people to think about the great values because they're watching TV. So the media *are* reaching vulnerable people who, from our standpoint, do not give attention to other things. With that huge slice of attention, then, goes responsibility for our values. And what values are they serving?

Empiricus: I was coming to that. When you talk about "serving" values, rather than changing or debasing them, you are on solider ground. To put the matter in too unqualified a way (but for the sake of brevity), the studies do seem to say that the mass media form or originate values hardly at all, they change or convert values only seldom, they shape or mold values somewhat but not very much, *but* they do a great deal to express, articulate, activate, reflect, and in short reinforce the dominant values already in existence.

Academicus: If that is so, what hope is there for the intellectual improvement and moral education of man? It all sounds to me like the reinforcement of the individual's bias and prejudice, forged in the bias and prejudice of his class, his religious affiliation, even the accident of his regional location.

Empiricus: Well, if that is indeed how it is — which is simply a question of fact — don't blame me. As one of your heroes long ago remarked, the one who asks the question should not be held responsible for the answer.

Practicus: But that is not a sufficient reply to Academicus. He seems to think there is something basically wrong in all this. I'm not sure at all. Why should change of belief be any more desirable in itself than stability of belief? When phrased in such neutral terms the obvious response is: Why indeed? What is reasonable stability to me is stubbornness to you, and what is reasonable change to you is vacillation to me. For my part, I like social stability: surely in itself that is as important as social change, and there can be little doubt that the media contribute to it. But is nothing worth conserving?

Academicus: Of course there is, but not what you are conserving via the media. They tend to reflect and reinforce the going values by telling us, as a society, what we most want to hear. What all of us most want to hear is how great and good and right we are; how justice triumphs, at least in the end; how good and evil are easily recognized; how rewarding it is to do one's duty; how pleasant and easy and full of fun life really is. To a major extent the mass media help us to indulge such global fantasies without recalling us sufficiently to the realities, the complexities, and the seriousness of life.

With regard to national stereotypes of a social character,

the notion of a country dominated and run by the "pure Americans" is reinforced, probably unconsciously, by the cast of characters in the short stories in the popular magazines: there the Anglo-Saxon and Nordic Protestants get the top roles and the top rewards, and the representatives of the minority groups get what is left. In women's magazines and radio's daytime serials, the good and noble wives and mothers, however poorly treated, are understanding, forgiving, and in the end triumphant.

Empiricus: Hold on a moment. You are now quoting from our own research. I thought you maintained the posture that empirical research was of little or no use in clarifying these value problems.

Academicus: I quote it when it agrees with me.

Empiricus: There you are. When it disagrees with you, you ignore it and it doesn't affect you. So your position doesn't *learn,* it just gets reinforced — precisely like the people I am talking about in mass audiences. But go on.

Academicus: As to personal values, they too find their reflection and resonance in the mass media. Sincerity is a treasured value in personal relations, and in view of the sophisticated slickness of the media and the manipulative intent of advertising it is no wonder that what passes for sincerity in the mass media is also treasured. Thus, Kate Smith could sell war bonds because of her apparent sincerity, and this plain-shoe element also accounts for the success of such figures as Ed Sullivan and Arthur Godfrey. (It is hard to think what else it might be!) Thus even sincerity has become marketable. So you can see that this runs pretty deep.

Take the familiar example: the value of adjustment. The experts tell us that if one shift in American values in recent decades is more pronounced, certain, and important than any other, it is the movement from the Puritan ethic of individualism, work, and a sense of independent righteousness to something like Riesman's other-directed man or Whyte's Organization Man for whom "good human relations" and "social adjustment" is the ultimate good — or even, since he seeks to move others, the ultimate weapon. As for the conflict and suffering and violence on television and in the movies, that comes only from the outside, and in black-and-white terms. The characters are not so much torn from within as subject to buffeting from without — from the gangster, the rustlers, the communists, or other villains. Gary Cooper can get shot in the leg, but no one can ever puncture his soul.

Practicus: That was typically eloquent of you, but also, I fear, typically immoderate. I could spend a lot of time simply correcting you on the facts but since you would probably consider that an attempt to evade the main point of your remarks, I will content myself merely with entering on the record my conviction — no, my knowledge — that the content of the mass media is much more varied than you suggest and that substantial parts of it are much more elevating. Considering how little time you have to give to such things, there's even enough for you!

Empiricus: You are too moderate in criticizing his immoderateness. Let me quote a serious scholar, Edward Shils, on the body of criticism of mass culture of which Academicus has just given us a sample:

> The critical interpretation of mass culture rests on a distinctive image of modern man, of modern society, and of man in past ages. This image has little factual basis. It is a product of disappointed political prejudices, value aspirations for an unrealizable ideal, resentment against American society, and at bottom, romanticism dressed up in the language of sociology, psychoanalysis, and existentialism. . . . The major error of the analysts of popular culture is their belief that it has succeeded to something which was intrinsically worthy, that man has sunk into a hitherto unknown mire because of it, and that this is a necessary prelude to the further degradation, and perhaps ultimate extinction, of high culture. . . .

It would be far more correct to assume that mass culture is now less damaging to the lower classes than the dismal and harsh existence of earlier centuries had ever been. The reading of good books, the enjoyment of superior music and painting, although perhaps meager, is certainly more widespread now than in previous centuries, and there is no reason to believe that it is less profound or less genuine. Only the frustrated attachment to an impossible ideal of human perfection, and a distaste for one's own society and for human beings as they are, can obscure this.[1]

This quotation comes from Shils' brilliant essay on "Daydreams and Nightmares: Reflections on the Criticism of Mass Culture," in which he also points out that "it is not accidental that most of the recent critics of mass culture are, or were, Marxian socialists (whose) earlier economic criticism of the capitalist society has been transformed into a moral and cultural criticism of the large-scale industrial society."

Practicus: You and Shils are making the same point I mentioned earlier. The critics don't like the society as it is, and want to change it. That is their privilege, and I must say that I often agree with them. But most of the main society does not agree and we managers of the media should not be asked to try to force the changes on an unwilling society. Besides, I can't. Values are typically formed where they should be: first in the home, then in the school and the church. Even in a society as rapidly changing as ours, the media cannot be charged with the responsibility of bringing about the conditions of the good life if the primary institutions have become unwilling or unable to do so. Let me quote Frank Stanton, the president of an enlightened broadcasting network:

> . . . I know where television will fail, and where it *has* to fail. It *has* to fail in substituting itself for an active participation in life itself. . . . We can help education, but we can-

---

[1] See Edward A. Shils (1957).

not *be* education. We can give the pulpit a wider range, but we cannot *be* religion. We can help the American home, but we cannot *be* parents.

Empiricus: However, if you managers of mass culture are taking the time and attention that used to go to familial discourse and the church, then you cannot escape the responsibility of the institutions whose role you are in part pre-empting. But I do agree in the case of educational institutions. There is a great deal of evidence to the effect that reading and listening on matters of cultural interest or aesthetic taste or public affairs or moral positions is inextricably bound up with level of education. Without rather advanced formal schooling, people don't go to the media for such things. It follows, I think, that the level of the media is directly dependent upon the level of popular education. That is why they are better today in this country than they ever were, why they are still limited today, but also why they will certainly be better tomorrow.

Academicus: That seems to me, as a professional educator, like the typical evasion in which the schools end up with all the blame. But we in education know, even if you don't, that our fate rests with the quality of the family, the community, and ultimately the nation. We can't do the whole job of persuading children to value the right things — especially when the parents fall down on the job because they are watching television instead! It is the familiar vicious circle: You mass-media people create a climate unfavorable to an interest in serious education and then tell us that you can't change that until we produce a mass audience that demands serious educational fare from the media.

Practicus: What always impresses me in discussions with you intellectuals is that it is I who turn out to be the historian. Somehow, when you approach this particular subject, you lose your sense of perspective, of historical balance, and you become the most weary of Utopia-seekers.

When has popular culture ever been free of violence, of heroes and villains, of romance, of happy endings — in short, when has it not been escape? Has what you call real life ever been so full of happiness for the masses of the people — or the elite either, for that matter — that they did not need to find a happier existence to dream about, and in, for a time? Folk tales and fairy tales have always been used to soften the harsh facts of life: everyone turns out to live happily ever after. Leaving aside the fact — and it is one, I'm convinced — that throughout history there have never been so many people participating in culture as today (and partly through the mass media) — leaving that aside, there is still the point that a number of important social functions are performed by the very stuff you like least. Violence in TV Westerns may be bad, but it's better than bear-baiting and carousing; and who knows, the psychologists who think that it draws off aggressive impulses that would otherwise express themselves more harmfully may be right. And what of recreation, in the literal sense of being re-created for another day's activities; who does not need that? If the general run of men do live lives of quiet desperation, there must be times when they can remove themselves from reality awhile to hear a story. Anyway, they always have.

Academicus: But that argument too is an evasion. It is always easy, on any human problem, to say that things were just as bad before. But that surely is less an argument to justify a do-nothing policy than it is a reason to do something. If it isn't novel but is still a problem, all the more need to do something about it. We sometimes think that this is a relatively new matter, but listen to what Kierkegaard said over 100 years ago:

> . . . communication has just about reached the lowest point, with respect to its importance; and contemporaneously the means of communication have pretty nearly attained the highest point, with respect to quick and overwhelming distribution. For what is in such haste to get out, and on the

other hand what has such widespread distribution as . . . twaddle? Oh procure silence.[2]

Has there been any progress since?

Practicus: To me, your quotation simply proves that you intellectuals are professional viewers-with-alarm, and always have been. Let me try once more to play the role of the historian.

What you fellows don't seem to appreciate is where you are in history — so let me tell you. You are at the point of trying to learn for the first time how to make a democratic mass culture work. All three aspects, the mass, the democratic, and the culture, make for difficulties in the operation of the media. The mass means heterogeneity and difference — you can't please everybody. The democratic means that the voter, that is, the audience, counts — you have to please somebody. The culture means that you have to please with something that counts, in political or aesthetic or ethical terms.

You fellows usually make two arguments. The first is that the media should be better for the sake of other people — that is, that *they* should be given what *you* like. But what does it matter if the media gaineth culture but loseth their audience? As Stanton said, "Any mass medium will always have to cater to the middle grounds that are always the most widely held, or cease to be. This is not a plot but a quotient!" I don't say that facetiously, nor crudely, as a justification for anything. I do seriously mean that just as you are entitled to your taste, so other people are entitled to theirs; and not only can't you impose yours in the short run, but you shouldn't either. And I grant that yours is better, though at the same time I'm not sure that applying elite standards to popular culture is legitimate — or rather, I'm sure it isn't.

Your second argument is that the media should be better for you. But think of the problem in terms of the familiar economic concept of the division of labor — increased efficiency due

[2] See Soren Kierkegaard (1940).

to specialization of function. What about a similar division of leisure? What I mean is this: the intellectuals have their own media of communication — high-brow books, literary and political journals of every shade and degree of opinion, classical records, art movies, and so on — and that system has worked quite well. Change the mass media over to that prescription and you will not only unsatisfy a large number of people but you will kill off some of the present specialized channels. All that would do is shift the intellectual audience from one source to another and leave the mass audience unfulfilled altogether.

In short, if you want the benefits of a democratic mass culture you have to pay the costs, too. This is one of the costs, that there are now whole classes of people who in earlier times would either have been told what to do or have been disregarded, but who must now be taken into account as equals, not only in political terms but in cultural terms as well.

(Academicus tries to reply, but Empiricus demands the floor.)

Empiricus: Let me speak, because I know what you both are going to say, but I can say it faster, and for both of you, because I have heard the script many times before, and always to the same impasse. You, Practicus, are going to say that you should give the public what it wants, under the banner of democracy. Then you, Academicus, will reply that that argument is specious since the market isn't really free: that the people like simply what is given them and that they would like it just as well if it were better. Then you will say, how do you know; you will say, why don't we try something different; you will reply that it's too risky — and there the matter will rest.

For my part, I agree with Edward Shils, who has said many things that needed saying in the article to which we referred earlier. On this point, for example:

There are certainly limitations in what the producers and

authors can accomplish because their employers are often convinced that only intellectual and esthetic products which we regard as inferior will find a large audience; there are probably also inherent limitations in the capacity of the audiences in the working and middle classes to respond appreciatively to works of good quality. It is far from certain, however, that the range of those limits has definitely been established and the best possible has been done within them.

This poses a central question — to my mind, perhaps *the* central question — in the great debate on the operation of the mass media from the standpoint of human values. That question is: how good can it be without losing its audience? It cannot lose its audience because the entire economic arrangement of the communications system depends upon audiences and I know of no alternative that would be as acceptable. The answer to the question is: no one knows. I have often thought that one day there should be a large-scale natural experiment in which a community would be systematically offered a rich and worthy communication diet over a sufficiently long time so that careful measurement against an appropriate control could determine how much it would take. Such a plan, it seems to me, meets the powerful market argument head-on: would another and better market do as well? It is too much to ask the media to risk everything on what is, after all, a problematic matter; but it is perhaps not too much to ask, as we are accustomed to in science, for the critical experiment.

Practicus: The trouble with you social scientists is that you see only your side of the problem. Consider, for example, our problem of talent. There is just not enough creative artistic and intellectual talent in the world to fill the mass media, with their tremendous needs for material. You can hardly fill the pages of your little quarterlies with stuff you respect. Think of the national weeklies, the hundreds of movies, the thousands of hours of radio and television: where is all that excellence to come from? And how is it all going to be paid for? If by government, you run grave dangers of political control. If by subscription, you will end up with today's shows — at a price.

Academicus: But you always think in terms of entertainment. What I am talking about, and speaking for, is values. What values do we want a communication system to promote and, we hope, realize? That is easy: clarification of political issues, stimulation of high esthetic taste, provision of moral and ethical debate, concern with the basic and tragic ends of human existence — nothing less, in short, than furtherance of the essential dignity of man. The media do not present to us the tragic character of life, nor its glories, but only its unrealities, its superficialities, its trivialities. In short, they do not help to illuminate the human condition.

Again let me quote the comments of a social scientist on the matter. In his fine book on *Responsibility in Mass Communications,* Will Schramm urges the media to stop treating the mass audience as either children or fools:

> It is unsafe (the media seems to feel) to let the Popular Arts man hear or see anything which might arouse elemental emotion. It is dangerous to expose him to anything which might test his faith in the sanctity of the marriage or the home, or in his religion, or in law or justice; he might fail the test. It is dangerous also to let him hear anything profane or vulgar; he might pick it up. More important, it is useless to expect him to respond to any very deep and insightful treatment of human nature and human life; instead he must be expected to respond only at a superficial level, only on the level of what is funny. . . . In these respects the Popular Arts Man is a child. In other respects he is a fool, for the media seem to assume that they can attract him by violence and sex, and then cover up the sex and punish the violence so that he won't see it or at least won't find it attractive.

Or take a philosophical view. In his inaugural lecture at Cambridge a few years ago, C. S. Lewis argued that the Great

Divide in Western culture came not between Antiquity and the Dark Ages, not between the Dark Ages and the Middle Ages, not with the rise of science at the end of the seventeenth century, but only in the last 150 years or so, between us and the age of Austen and Scott. He rests his argument on differences in politics, the arts, and religion, and on the birth of the machine and its psychological effects. And though he did not say so, the communication system is now at the root of the great changes that have taken place, affecting the conduct and image of politics and religion, the standards by which we judge the arts, and the respect we give to the machines. But it is not living up to its responsibilities for the furtherance of human values, and that is my criticism.

Practicus: But in a society as complex and varied as this, it is not easy to know what values to communicate. The difficulty with using one's basic values as a guide to decision is that it settles only the decisions that are easy. The hard decisions, and the important ones, are precisely those in which values are split, some on one side and some on the other, so that the appraisal of means to ends is truly agonizing. For example, looking at the matter from the value standpoint, the generality and uniformity of the media complement very well the heterogeneity and fragmentation of the society: the media tie the country together by focusing our attention on the same things at the same time, while all our social, religious, ideological, economic, and regional distinctions are pulling in different and often conflicting directions. And the unity of values that exists amid the diversity derives primarily from symbols. And I must say that I prefer this softening of differences to the dogmatism and certainty and even arrogance of earlier eras.

Anyway, it certainly is not self-evident to me that valued things must always be such serious things. You cannot ask the mass media to do nothing but educate, clarify, enrichen, deepen, analyze, moralize, and elevate. Man does not live by bread alone; he needs circuses, too. If the media were always deadly serious, they would be deadly, and in not very long, dead as well.

_____

And so the argument would run. We like to think: *De gustibus non est disputandum.* But there really is nothing to dispute *but* tastes (i.e., values), and our spokesmen have been diligent in putting forward their respective points of view, as fairly as I could do so in the time available. And they have been put forward in juxtaposition, rather than in isolation, where each camp normally talks only to itself. Here there has been at least the attempt to force the proponents of the three positions to communicate, to argue out their assumptions and to face the facts and problems of the others, to attack and defend, in short, to debate together the great issues of cultural democracy.

What does the confrontation come to, in the end? What should we learn from it?

First, and foremost: however attractive and persuasive each position is by itself, none really stands up in the face of sustained criticism from the others. Once the arguments of each side are assembled and set down together, they not only begin to war with one another, but at least in my judgment, they score points so that no one emerges unscathed or victorious. And I believe these are central and genuine positions; so I trust that you will not consider all this as simply an exercise in applied strawmanship.

If the positions cannot stand up to one another, why is that so? Primarily, I think, simply because they have not had to. They exist, for the most part, in their own worlds — as far apart as a Madison Avenue public relations talk, an editorial in an *avant-garde* literary magazine, and a sociological research paper. There is, of course, no reason why each side should not play its own tune as sweetly and as loudly as it likes, but there is every reason for them to enter into a serious struggle for survival. And that has not occurred. If it had, the positions would not now be so vulnerable to one another's criticisms; more would have rubbed off from the other sides; we would see more meeting of minds, more accommodation and synthesis and taking-into-account than we now do. In a sense, the participants act as though they still consider this a game — a game to be played with one's own rules, one's own cheering section, and one's own referees, but not in the same arena.

But the new cultural democracy is raising the same kinds of problems now that were raised in their day by political, educational, and economic democracy and requires that same kind of sustained and responsible debate over a period of years before its problems will be, if not solved, then clarified and defined and appreciated for what they are. As I read about the evolution of political democracy in this country, the debaters were seriously trying to persuade one another, not merely score points, in the effort to get workable formulations that would *survive* criticism and shape the new state. Of course there were the doctrinaires, the equivalent today of commercial people in New York and Hollywood who *know* that "nothing else will work" and intellectuals who *know* that their own brand of cultural change will solve everyone's problems. But the major figures of political democracy are major precisely because they did something practical to solve some of the emerging problems.

What we do not need is more glib statements of position by the various sides — statements for the record, and little else. Simply to berate the mass media for not being better or for not being what one personally wants them to be is worse than useless — worse because it corrupts the debate, contaminates the atmosphere, and sets the sides against one another in more intransigent array than is required by the situation. Simply to defend the mass media against any criticism or suggestion or question is similarly bad, and for the same reasons. As I have tried to show by our hypothetical conversation, there is already enough of that.

What we do need, I think, is the responsible joining of the issue and the search, together, for devices and mechanisms and ideas that have a chance of improving the situation. Not "solving" it: that asks too much too soon, and is itself an evasion and escape, on both sides. What is needed is the invention and perfection, for the problems of cultural democracy, of the counterparts of juries, supreme courts, school boards, referenda, labor unions and similar devices that now seem natural as a result of the earlier "great debates," but took a great deal of ingenuity and persistence to come by in the first place. We do not even have the proper institutions in which to discuss the problems together in a dispassionate manner — as this hypothetical debate shows.

To conclude, then, the points that Academicus, Practicus, and Empiricus can make *seem* good, but only because they aim at seeming, at appearances. They are what are called "good public relations" on Madison Avenue and good "theoretical lines" in protest magazines and learned journals. They may be good arguments in a point-scoring dispute, but they are not good platforms for reasonable negotiation. They are vulnerable one to the other so that they checkmate each other. They are not directly involved in the kind of competitive elimination, modification, and adjustment by which, in history, serious men have honestly worked out their differences into a workable system better than what they had.

We need to take the debate on cultural democracy seriously, for we are at a historical point in its development. If we cannot learn how to control and channel the strength of mass culture, we shall nonetheless have to live with it, for it is here and there is no way to turn it off.

*Thomas J. Stritch is Associate Professor
and head of the Department of Communication
Arts, University of Notre Dame; has been a member
of the editorial staffs of the* Nashville Banner *and*
South Bend Tribune; *contributor to* What America Stands For,
*1959; active in many professional organizations, including
the Association for Education in Journalism, the
Catholic Press Association, and others.*

Thomas J. Stritch

COMMUNICATIONS CRITICISM

AND ARTISTIC CHANGE

SOME OF MY COLLEAGUES MAY THINK ME INCAPABLE OF agreement, but in this case they must recognize a certain moral necessity. For Bernard Berelson says many things they have heard me trying to say for some years, only much better. He pays his respects, in a footnote, to Henry Murray and William McPhee for his form; but I see in its felicity a harking back to an older writer, much neglected these days, whose good sense was matched by his delight in dialogue argument, and whose mind was free to take the side reason plus autonomy indicated. I mean Thomas Love Peacock, and I can pay the present author no higher compliment than to so link him. To the pleasures of agreement, then, I must add, in the happy title of the portable edition, the Pleasures of Peacock.

If it is my place to add a fourth to the preceding debate's triumvirate, I would have to be named Secundus. I take Berelson's own central point — as opposed to those of Academicus, Empiricus and Practicus — to be that his paper is one of those "impossible interviews." In real life these three don't meet, don't debate, don't know one another — at least not well enough for the debate to get off the ground. If it had, I quote him for emphasis, "the positions would not now be so vulnerable to one another's criticism; more would have rubbed off from the other sides; we would see more meeting of minds, more accommodation and synthesis and taking-into-account than we do now." In these words, and by this position, Berelson is noting the odd claustrophobia of occupations and groups in American life, the sense of isolation and insulation that seals off advertising art from fine art, historians from journalists, jazz from long-hair, economists from sociologists, town from gown, lawyers from bureaucrats, Catholics from Mormons, Republicans from Democrats, and television repairmen from everybody.

Early in the paper Empiricus notes that the mass media have only a slight effect on American life, that they do not create or alter values but only reinforce those already held. I suggest that *insulation* is one of the main reasons for this. It isn't that we don't cross group lines — we are notoriously friendly — but when we do, we don't take our beliefs with us, to test and strengthen them in debate and trial. Consequently, our beliefs are not so much strongly held, as Empiricus says, but tightly held, privately cherished, passed back and forth only among the initiate, like family pride and family heirlooms. We have the most advanced communications network in the world. And the world's system is so advanced that a tremor of response nearly anywhere, especially in the free world, is magnified and transmitted along its nervous lines and quivering antennae until the whole world feels the shock. With all this we choose, or are forced to communicate only that little stock of what is commonly held and felt, the surface patter and chatter of life, not its shaping ideas and forces.

I think Practicus would add here that the media oppose this least common denominator tendency more than anyone would suppose. Actually the media propose and discuss more ideas and ideals, set up more confrontations of opposing viewpoints, than is normally done in everyday life. This may still not be enough to suit Academicus, but Practicus insists that the media can't get too far from the norms of everyday life. The American whom John Hutchison described previously does not like strong convictions. Bishop Sheen is popular with him for what he has in common with Pat Boone, not for his Catholicism; one learns with surprise of Boone's own Protestantism; the *Christian Science Monitor* is celebrated for anything but its Christian Science; there should be a prize for describing the politics of the *New York Times* or the *Milwaukee Journal;* and it was television that ruined Joe McCarthy. Indeed, both media and persons who hold strong positions — John Foster Dulles, the *National Review,* the *Brooklyn Tablet,* the *Nation,* Cyrus Eaton, Casey Stengel, Howard Hughes — are regarded as somewhat suspicious, so chary are Americans of proclaiming their convictions, or so lacking are they in having any.

"Other-directedness, superficiality and thinness in personal relations, interest in personality rather than character — such tendencies may very well have been accelerated and reinforced by the mass media," says Academicus. Empiricus answers yes, perhaps. Secundus, for once, says no. I have long felt that the deep implications of Riesman's famous work are basically religious. Lack of direction, of orientation of the work of living, loss of ideals of holiness or strength, uncertainty about values — these are the marks of the culture which John Hutchison has described in his analysis, one that, despite an increase in religious affiliation, has no strong, difference-making faith. No wonder this is reflected in the mass media. But to blame the mass media for the culture it reflects is like blaming Desdemona's handkerchief for Iago's devil and Othello's tragic flaw.

But I would like to revert to my role of Secundus, and try to elaborate Berelson's thesis in a different direction. He is careful not to impute any special blame to any one of his three protagonists; however, I think, from the nature of the case, Academicus gets the major share, simply because he is the more broadly responsible person. Not the first, yet surely one of the major functions of the intellectual is to search for the common ground where an issue may be joined. Though his special function is to transcend the common life, yet still he shares it with all levels of his countrymen, and in a healthy society he rejoices in the folkways and folk art. This is, I think, not generally true of the American intellectual.

FOLK ART TO FINE ART

One of the most striking features in American culture is that folk art very rarely crosses the line into fine art. One might almost say this is the normal path to fine art. The melodies of Beethoven and Brahms are German folk tunes. The quartets of Bartok are the fruit of his research into Hungarian folk music. The art of Goya, Daumier, Delacroix, Lautrec, Grosz, to name only a few, is the art of the poster and cartoon grown great; even the great wall paintings of the Renaissance are in some splendid and incredible and marvellous sense, illustrated biblical folk tales. Much literature is folk story grown great — Homer, Chaucer, Dostoevski, Tolstoy, Hardy, Kafka, Wordsworth, Balzac, Yeats, to name a bare handful.

Now, in the United States there is an abundant source of folk stuff, rather more, I think, than in most countries. There are the Indian stories and dances, the legends of the West, the tremendous store of Negro story and song, the hymns of the camp meetings, the folkways of special groups like the Shakers and the Mormons, heroic legends like Bunyan's and Crockett's, minstrel shows, vaudeville, jazz, square dancing, national games like baseball, heaven knows what all. But how little of this has been transmuted into fine art! And how thin are many of the attempts — *Baby Doe, Porgy and Bess, Merry Mount, The Big Sky, Shane, Ramona* — the list is not a distinguished one. There was a revealing television program on this point a short time ago, of the kind Academicus would, I hope, approve: Leonard Bernstein's analysis of Gershwin's *Rhapsody in Blue,* an attempt to bring jazz over into fine art, disparaged in comparison with *La Création du Monde* which did the same thing. And it was written by Darius Milhaud, a Frenchman.

A similar case can be made in journalism. The European intellectual turns naturally to journalism; his American counterpart tends to stay in the Academy. One thinks of Mauriac, of Shaw, of Churchill, of Siegfried, of Malraux, of Chesterton, of Sartre, of de Jouvenel, of Weber, of Naumann, of Waldemar Gurian, journalists and intellectuals, publicists yet originators of ideas. Their counterparts in the United States are few indeed.

But the most telling feature, rather failure, in my opinion, was the American film. Here we had everything going for us — the inventions themselves, the great early artists like Griffith, Chaplin and Fairbanks, the best craftsmen, world domination, oodles of money. Yet I think even the most avid film fan, like myself, would concede that the American film never made the grade into truly fine, or truly national, art. This transition was made successfully by Italian opera in the nineteenth century, which began as the most conventional of mass entertainment and flowered into the work of Rossini, Bellini and Verdi, with all levels of the population participating in its enjoyment and fulfilling themselves in its artistic splendor and success.

Of course I do not suggest that Academicus must answer for all this, if, indeed, there is anything to answer for. It may be that our culture is more Babylonian than Greek. But I do say that Academicus historically did very little to help our folk art over the hump. His attitude was and is precisely what he so righteously and damningly accuses his adversaries of: lack of interest and help. He complains that there is not enough of his sort of thing in the mass media; to quote him, "clarification of political issues, stimulation of high esthetic taste, provision for moral and ethical debate, concern with the basic and tragic ends of human existence — nothing less, in short, than furtherance of the essential dignity of man." To which the record answers that he has neglected the most obvious path to many of these excellent goals: the promise that lies in the deep-seated wisdom and esthetic experience of the life around him. The shepherd of Virgil, Dr. Johnson tells us, grew at last acquainted with love and found him a native of the rocks. We can learn much from the English in this respect, who prefer their own thoughts and arts even when they are admittedly not very good, like their cooking.

Berelson builds his argument around the idea of the debate about cultural democracy. He will concede, I fancy, that Practicus does not hesitate to vulgarize the folk arts and debase folk wisdom, if that will sell his soap. And it may be that Empiricus travels the long way round, like Virgil's shepherd, to get home to the values of common sense, good family and communal life. But these at least cannot get very far from their culture. Academicus has done a good deal to repudiate it. He is, of all our groups, one of the most inbred — his psychology, Professor Seymour Lipset says, is like that of the coal miner; and like the miner's son, D. H. Lawrence, he yearns beyond the seas, spurning the life that nurtured him.

This is a good life, if we believe, and I firmly do, the testimony of Father Fitzpatrick and Professor Williams. And I believe too that the problems raised by Professors Kluckhohn and Kolb, ultimately philosophical in nature, signify some breakdown of that sense of isolation I have spoken of. Many human students dislike what Professor Hutchison calls "the language of values"; I once did myself. But their serious and competent discussion suggests that the behavioral sciences and sociology in particular are now returning to their great European beginnings. As Father Ward has recently said in the *Review of Politics,* it is in this way that such disciplines transcend their self-defeating positivism and lay claim to real universality. It is the greatest merit of these discussions, may I say as its last formal speaker, to have testified to this.

BIBLIOGRAPHY

Adler, Franz. "The Value Concept in Sociology." *American Journal of Sociology,* 62:272-79, 1956.

Albert, Ethel M., and Kluckhohn, Clyde. *A Selected Bibliography on Values, Ethics and Esthetics in the Behavioral Sciences and Philosophy, 1920-1958.* Glencoe: Free Press, 1959.

American Council on Education. *Long Range Planning for Education.* Washington, D.C.: American Council on Education, 1958.

Anshen, R. N. (ed.). *Moral Principles of Action.* New York: Harper and Brothers, 1952.

Argyris, Chris. *Personality and Organization.* New York: Harper and Brothers, 1957.

Bakke, E. Wight. *Mutual Survival: The Goal of Unions and Management.* New York: Harper and Brothers, 1947.

Becker, Howard. *Through Values to Social Interpretation; Essays on Social Contexts, Actions, Types and Prospects.* Durham: Duke University Press, 1950.

Bell, Daniel. *The New American Right.* New York: Criterion Books, 1955.

————. *Work and Its Discontents.* Boston: Beacon Press, 1956.

Berelson, Bernard, Lazarsfeld, Paul F., and McPhee, William N. *Voting: A Study of Opinion Formation in a Presidential Campaign.* Chicago: University of Chicago Press, 1954.

————, and Salter, Patricia J. "Majority and Minority Americans: An Analysis of Magazine Fiction." *Public Opinion Quarterly,* 10:168-90, 1947.

Bloch, Bernard. "On Contrast." *Language,* 29:59-61, 1953.

Bogart, Leo. *The Age of Television.* New York: Frederick Ungar Publications, 1956.

Boulding, Kenneth E. *The Organizational Revolution.* New York: Harper and Brothers, 1953.

Bowen, Howard R. *Social Responsibilities of the Business Man.* New York: Harper and Brothers, 1953.

————, et al. *Ethics and Economic Life.* New York: Harper and Brothers, 1954.

Brim, Orville G. *Sociology and the Field of Education.* New York: Russell Sage Foundation, 1958.

Childs, Marquis and Cater, Douglas. *Ethics in a Business Society.* New York: Harper and Brothers, 1954.

Cronin, John. *Catholic Social Principles.* Milwaukee: Bruce Publishing Co., 1950.

Cuber, John, Harper, Robert, and Kenkel, William. *Problems of American Society: Values in Conflict.* Third Edition. New York: Henry Holt, 1956.

Dahlke, Otto H. *Values in Culture and Classroom: A Study of the Sociology of the School.* New York: Harper and Brothers, 1958.

Delesalle, Jacques. *Liberté et valeur.* Louvain: Publications universitaires de Louvain, 1950.

Deploige, Simon. *Le conflit de la morale et de la sociologie.* Second edition. Paris: Nouvelle libraire nationale, 1912.

Drucker, Peter. *America's Next Twenty Years.* New York: Harper and Brothers, 1957.

————. *The New Society.* New York: Harper and Brothers, 1949.

Durkheim, Emile. "Cours de science sociale." *Revue internationale de l'Enseignement,* 13:313-38 and 423-40, 1904.

Eisenstadt, S. N. "Communications Systems and Social Structure: An Exploratory Comparative Study." *Public Opinion Quarterly,* 19:152-67, 1955.

Fanfani, A. *Catholicism, Capitalism and Protestantism.* New York: Sheed and Ward, 1946.

Farnsworth, Dana L. "Emotions and Learning." *Harvard Educational Review,* 25:95-104, 1955.

Fichter, Joseph. *Social Relations in the Urban Parish.* Chicago: University of Chicago Press, 1954.

————. *Sociology.* Chicago: University of Chicago Press, 1957.

————. "Religion: Integrator of the Culture." *Thought,* 13:361-82, 1958.

————. *Religion as an Occupation: A Study in the Sociology of Professions.* Notre Dame: University of Notre Dame Press, 1961.

Finkelstein, Louis. "The Business Man's Moral Failure." *Fortune,* 58:116-17, 1958.

Firth, Raymond. *Elements of Social Organization.* New York: Philosophical Library, 1951.

Fitch, John A. *Social Responsibilities of Organized Labor.* New York: Harper and Brothers, 1957.

Fitzpatrick, Joseph P. "American Achievement." *Catholic Mind,* 56:42-50, 1956.

Foote, Nelson, "Identification as a Theory of Motivation." *American Sociological Review,* 16:14-21, 1951.

Form, William H. and Miller, Delbert. *Industry, Labor and Community.* New York: Harper and Brothers, 1960.

Fortune editors. "U. S. A. The Permanent Revolution." *Fortune,* 43:61-212, 1951.

Frank, Lawrence K. *The School as Agent for Cultural Renewal.* Cambridge: Harvard University Press, 1959.

Frankel, Charles. *The Case for Modern Man.* Boston: Beacon Press, 1959.

Fraser, L. M. *Economic Thought and Language.* New York: John Wiley and Sons, 1937.

Fromm, Eric. *The Sane Society.* New York: Rinehart, 1955.

Furfey, Paul H. *Scope and Method of Sociology.* New York: Harper and Brothers, 1953.

Galbraith, John. *The Affluent Society.* Boston: Houghton Mifflin, 1958.

Gerth, H. H. and Mills, C. W. "A Marx for Managers." *Ethics,* 52:200-15, 1942.

Gilliland, A. R. "Changes in Religious Beliefs of College Students." *Journal of Social Psychology,* 37:113-16, 1953.

Glock, Charles Y. *Toward a Typology of Religious Orientation.* New York: Bureau of Applied Social Research, Columbia University, 1954.

Herberg, Will. *Protestant-Catholic-Jew.* Garden City: Doubleday, 1955.

Hertzler, Joyce O. *Society in Action.* New York: Dryden, 1954.

Himmelweit, Hilde T., Oppenheim, A. N., and Vince, Pamela. *Television and the Child.* New York: Oxford University Press, 1958.

Householder, F. W., Jr. Review of *Studies Presented to Joshua Whatmough. Language,* 34:398-408, 1958.

Hutchison, John A. *Faith, Reason and Existence.* New York: Oxford University Press, 1956.

Janis, Irving L., *et al. Personality and Persuasibility.* New Haven: Yale University Press, 1959.

Katz, Elihu and Lazarsfeld, Paul F. *Personal Influence: The Part Played by People in the Flow of Mass Communications.* Glencoe: The Free Press, 1955.

Katzell, Raymond A. "Is Individualism Disappearing?" *Harvard Business Review,* 36:139-52, 1958.

Keesing, Felix (ed.). *Anthropological Contributions to Value Theory.* Revised edition. Stanford: Stanford University Press, 1955.

Kernodle, R. Wayne. *The Sixth Decade of Our Century: The Developing Fabric of American Society.* Williamsburg: The College of William and Mary, 1959.

Kierkegaard, Soren. *The Present Age.* Translated by Alexander Dru and Walter Lowrie. New York: Oxford University Press, 1940.

Klapper, Joseph T. *The Effects of Mass Communication.* Glencoe: The Free Press, 1960.

Kluckhohn, Clyde. Toward a Comparison of Value-Emphases in Different Cultures. In: *The State of the Social Sciences,* edited by Leonard D. White. Chicago: University of Chicago Press, pp. 116-32, 1956.

————. The Scientific Study of Values. In: *Three Lectures.* Toronto: University of Toronto Press, pp. 25-54, 1959.

Kluckhohn, Florence and Strodtbeck, Fred. *Variations in Value Orientations.* Evanston: Row, Peterson, 1961.

Kolb, William. The Changing Prominence of Values in Modern Sociological Theory. In: *Modern Sociological Theory,* edited by H. Becker and A. Boskoff. New York: Dryden Press, 1957.

————. "Values, Positivism, and the Functional Theory of Religion; The Growth of a Moral Dilemma." *Social Forces,* 31:305-11, 1953.

Lazarsfeld, Paul F., Berelson, Bernard, and Gaudet, Hazel. *The People's Choice.* New York: Columbia University Press, 1948.

Lee, Dorothy. Culture and the Experience of Value. In: *New Knowledge in Human Values,* edited by A. Maslow. New York: Harper and Brothers, pp. 165-77, 1959.

Lerner, Max. *America As a Civilization.* New York: Simon and Schuster, 1957.

Loomis, Charles P., and Beegle, J. Allen. *Rural Sociology.* Englewood Cliffs: Prentice-Hall, 1957.

Lundberg, George. *Can Science Save Us?* New York: Longmans, Green, 1947.

————. "Science, Scientists and Values." *Social Forces,* 30:373-79, 1952.

MacLean, Otto H. *Scholars, Workers and Gentlemen.* Cambridge: Harvard University Press, 1958.

Mannheim, Karl. *Diagnosis of Our Time.* London: Kegan Paul, Trench, Trubner, 1943.

Mannoury, G. "On Two-Valued Polarities and Their Avoidance." *ETC.,* 7:203-208, 1950.

Maslow, Abraham (ed.). *New Knowledge in Human Values.* New York: Harper and Brothers, 1959.

Mayo, Elton. *Social Problems of an Industrial Civilization.* Cambridge: Harvard University Press, 1945.

Merton, Robert K. *Social Theory and Social Structure.* Glencoe: The Free Press, 1957.

Mills, C. Wright. *White Collar.* New York: Oxford University Press, 1951.

————. "The Powerless People: The Role of the Intellectual in Society." *Politics,* 1:68-72, 1944.

Moore, Wilbert. *Industrial Relations and the Social Order.* Revised edition. New York: Macmillan, 1951.

Morrison, Elting E. (ed.). *The American Style.* New York: Harper and Brothers, 1958.

Nisbet, Robert. *The Quest for Community.* New York: Oxford University Press, 1953.

Northrop, F. S. C. "Conflicts of Values in a Community of Cultures." *Journal of Philosophy,* 47:197-210, 1950.

Nottingham, Elizabeth K. *Religion and Society.* New York: Doubleday, 1954.

O'Dea, Thomas. *American Catholic Dilemma.* New York: Sheed and Ward, 1959.

———. "The Sociology of Religion." *American Catholic Sociological Review,* 15:73-103, 1954.

Parsons, Talcott, and Shils, Edward A. *Toward a General Theory of Action.* Cambridge: Harvard University Press, 1952.

———. *Essays in Sociological Theory: Pure and Applied.* Glencoe: The Free Press, 1949.

Pepper, Stephen C. *The Sources of Value.* Berkeley: University of California Press, 1958.

Perlman, Mark. *Labor Theories in America: Background and Development.* Evanston: Row, Peterson, 1958.

Repley, Ray (ed.). *Value Theory: A Cooperative Inquiry.* New York: Thomas Y. Crowell, 1949.

Rieff, Philip. Review of Durkheim's *Education and Society.* In: *American Sociological Review,* 22:233, 1957.

Riesman, David. *Individualism Reconsidered and Other Essays.* Glencoe: The Free Press, 1954.

———. *Constraint and Variety in American Education.* Lincoln: University of Nebraska Press, 1956.

———. *The Lonely Crowd.* New Haven: Yale University Press, 1950.

Riley, John W., and Riley, Matilda White. Mass Communication and the Social System. In: *Sociology Today: Problems and Prospects,* edited by Robert K. Merton, Leonard Broom and Leonard S. Cottrell, Jr. New York: Basic Books, 1959.

Rosenberg, Morris. *Occupations and Values.* Glencoe: The Free Press, 1952.

Rosenberg, Bernard, and White, David Manning. *Mass Culture, The Popular Arts in America.* Glencoe: The Free Press, 1957.

Schlichter, Sumner. *Trade Unions in a Free Society.* Cambridge: Harvard University Press, 1948.

Schramm, Wilbur (ed.). *Mass Communications, A Book of Readings.* Second edition. Urbana: University of Illinois Press, 1960.

———. *The Process and Effects of Mass Communication.* Urbana: University of Illinois Press, 1954.

Selekman, Sylvia K., and Selekman, Benjamin. *Power and Morality in a Business Society.* New York: McGraw-Hill, 1956.

Shils, Edward A. "Daydreams and Nightmares: Reflections on the Criticism of Mass Culture." *Sewanee Review,* 65:587-608, 1957.

———. "Primordial, Personal, Sacred and Civil Ties." *British Journal of Sociology,* 8:130-45, 1957.

Sjorbert, Gideon, and Cain, Leonard D., Jr. "Negative Values and Social Action." *Alpha Kappa Deltan,* 29:63-70, 1959.

Skinner, B. F. *Science and Human Behavior.* New York: Macmillan, 1953.

Speiser, E. A. "The Pitfalls of Polarity." *Language,* 14:187-202, 1938.
Spitz, Rene. *No and Yes. On the Genesis of Human Communication.* New York: International Universities Press, 1957.
Staley, Eugene (ed.). *Creating an Industrial Civilization.* New York: Harper and Brothers, 1952.
Sutton, Francis X., *et al. The American Business Creed.* Cambridge: Harvard University Press, 1956.
Tawney, R. *Religion and the Rise of Capitalism.* New York: Harcourt, Brace, 1926.
Vogt, Evon Z., and Roberts, John M. (eds.). *The Peoples of Rimrock: A Comparative Study of Value Systems.* Evanston: Row, Peterson, 1960.
Wallace, Anthony F. C., and Atkins, John. *The Logic and Application of Componential Analysis.* Mimeographed, n.d.
Ward, A. Dudley. *Goals of Economic Life.* New York: Harper and Brothers, 1952.
————, Leavy, Stanley, and Freedman, Lawrence. *The American Economy and the Lives of People.* New York: Harper and Brothers, 1953.
Ward, Leo R. (ed.). *Ethics and the Social Sciences.* Notre Dame: University of Notre Dame Press, 1959.
Weber, Christian O. *Basic Philosophies of Education.* New York: Rinehart, 1960.
Weber, Max. *The Methodology of the Social Sciences.* Translated and edited by Edward A. Shils and Henry A. Finch. Glencoe: The Free Press, 1949.
————. *The Protestant Ethic and the Spirit of Capitalism.* Translated by Talcott Parsons. New York: Scribner's, 1930.
Williams, Robin M., Jr. *American Society, A Sociological Interpretation.* (revised in 1960) New York: Knopf, 1951.
————. "Religion, Value-Orientations, and Inter-Group Conflict." *Journal of Social Issues,* 12:12-20, 1956.
Whyte, William H., Jr. *The Organization Man.* New York: Simon and Schuster, 1956.
Yinger, J. Milton. *Religion, Society and the Individual.* New York: Macmillan, 1957.